"If you've struggled to slow down b
a wheel that won't stop spinning, 7
is what you need right now. Author
nonstop struggle and she invites you   wiy slow is the
solution that you've been praying for. As you are inspired by Laura's
personal journey, are encouraged by Jesus's teaching, and learn
practical tools, you'll find success in allowing God's prescription
for slow to soothe your soul."

—**Barb Roose**, speaker and author of *Stronger Than Stress: Ten
Spiritual Practices to Win the Battle of Overwhelm* and others

"This book speaks to my soul with its reminders to take a breather,
lighten your load, and find rest in the chaos of everyday life.
From practical tips on how to slow down to deep reflections on
what truly matters, this book is like a gentle nudge in the right
direction. So if you're ready to hit pause, catch your breath, and
rediscover what's important in life, give this book a read. Trust
me, you won't regret it!"

—**Ashley Henriott**, Christ-based
confidence coach, author, and speaker

"Laura shows us how to take Jesus up on His offer to 'get away
with me and recover your life.' I've learned to expect Laura's
compelling vulnerability in her writing and this book does not
disappoint. But I didn't expect to feel such personal invitations
from Jesus through her words into the slower, sweeter life we are
all desperate for."

—**Alli Patterson**, teaching pastor at Crossroads Church
and author of *How to Stay Standing: 3 Essential
Practices for Building a Faith That Lasts*

"We live in a toxic hustle culture. No matter their age, everyone seems to be busy and our fast pace of life is slowly killing us. That is why Laura's book is not only timely but necessary. I love how she invites readers in with relatable personal stories and leads us to a place of understanding how to slow down practically."

—**Simi John**, Bible teacher and author of *I Am Not: Break Free from Stereotypes and Become the Woman God Made You to Be*

"This book is like sitting with a wise spiritual director—someone who knows the way and is willing to walk beside you as a guide when you can't see the full picture yourself. Laura has such an invitational way of writing that she makes slowing down, even in our fast paced world, attainable for every person reading. As a pastor, I agree with her plea. The need to slow down—the need for rhythms of life that protect people from burning out or burning down all that is good in life—is urgent. . . . I would highly recommend this book to anyone looking for a way to live fully instead of exhausted."

—**Kristan Dooley**, discipleship pastor of Anthem House Church and author of *Left Turns: Following Jesus Off the Beaten Path* and *Bigger: Rebuilding the Broken*

The Urgency of Slowing Down

Biblical Wisdom for Everyday Renewal

Laura L. Smith

Our Daily Bread
Publishing®

The Urgency of Slowing Down: Biblical Wisdom for Everyday Renewal
© 2024 by Laura L. Smith

Interior design by Michael J. Williams

ISBN,978-1-916718-45-6

Library of Congress Cataloging-in-Publication Data Available

Printed in the United Kingdom
24 25 26 27 28 29 30 31 / 8 7 6 5 4 3 2 1

To Brett, Maddie, Max, Mallory, and Maguire—
you are always worth slowing down for

Contents

Introduction
How It Started

I woke up next to my husband on a Saturday morning in March, rolled over, and checked my phone. 9:18 a.m.! I hadn't slept that late in years. And nothing in our life suggested this should be possible. In fact, we weren't even supposed to be in the same city this morning, let alone either of us sleeping in.

I was scheduled to be in Tennessee with one of our daughters at her soccer tournament. Our calendar placed my husband in Columbus, cheering on one of our sons who had advanced to the state level in his high school marketing competition. This is what our life looked like. Loads of wonderful events and meetings and conferences and tournaments and opportunities. Lots of divide and conquer. Not much sleep. Which equated to always feeling like we were running short on time and patience. We rarely gathered as a family under the same roof at the same time. We had no idea how frantic we were because we were in the eye of the hurricane, where there's an eerie disconnect with the actual frenetic spinning.

Then we got an email canceling the competition, followed by a text saying the soccer tournament was also called off. In the following hours and days, everything else on our jam-packed calendars was also deleted due to the COVID-19 pandemic.

Disappointment hung heavy in our house—over things we'd lost, over things not looking as we expected or hoped.

In an instant we had a slower life.

I'd been seeking some slowness in my life, but not very successfully. And when this all happened? Well, we didn't ease into it or plan it—it's just how things were. We didn't have to wake up at 5:45 a.m. to get the kids off to school because they were Zooming in on their laptops from their beds at 8:00 a.m. There was no sprinting out the door at 2:15 p.m. to pick up someone from school, get them to rehearsal, and then come home for a twenty-minute interlude to assemble some sort of grab-and-go dinner before heading out the door to someone else's away game. Instead, there was time to leisurely cook a dinner we could all sit down to eat together, walk around the neighborhood at sunset, maybe play a game or watch a movie when we returned. It was not only lovely but life-giving.

The frequent headaches I'd been getting disappeared. Amazing what a good night's sleep will do for you. Our family grew closer than we had been in years—we weren't all going our own directions at high speeds. We ate better. We did puzzles, baked cookies, told stories, went for strolls in the woods, worshiped as a family on the couch on Sunday mornings, read our Bibles on the porch. We felt more balanced. Sundays were extra slow and nourishing. We learned the benefits of braking and breaking.

Of course, there were plenty of struggles with the shutdown, but this slower rhythm was special. I felt God's presence in it. I had space in my head and heart to hear Him more clearly than I had in a long while. When the world ramped up again, I wanted to take the things I learned from the quiet life and infuse them into my routine.

And here we are. Back to a full schedule. My husband was out of town last weekend. I'll be gone two weeks from now. Two practices today. Tomorrow, which is Saturday, holds cross-country practice for one of our kids at 7:30 a.m., which means leaving our house at 6:45 a.m., followed by another kid's game at midday. And I love this life. I love seeing my kids do what lights them up inside. I love being there to cheer them on. I love the work my husband and I are called to, and I want to do it well. But I don't want to jump back into the hurricane.

I want to feel rested in my body and my soul. I want there to be enough quiet in my life to have time to talk to Jesus—really talk to Him—to walk with Jesus and truly listen to what He says. It's urgent for me to resist the frantic. It's urgent for me to hold on to the slow.

Jesus shows us this through His own life—one filled with getting away to be still and silent, waking early to pray, pulling away from the fray of the crowds: if we truly want to live, it's urgent for all of us to slow down.

It's urgent for all of us to slow down.

But do we?

I recently got a text in a group chat of friends that said, "Do any of you feel like the woman who spins plates on the top of sticks? I'm holding 37 sticks right now, or at least that's how I feel."

How many plates do you feel like you're spinning?

I don't want this frantic feeling of trying to keep it all together but fearing that at any moment it will all come tumbling down . . . for my friend, for myself, or for you. There's a better way.

God instructs in Psalm 46:10, "Be still, and know that I am God."

But when was the last time you stood still?

Really still.

For more than five minutes. Just quiet and alone with God. Your phone down, your TV off, and your laptop closed. And no, sleeping doesn't count.

It's urgent for us to slow down. For our bodies and our souls. We can do this. We need to for our physical, mental, and spiritual health. Jesus promises us the fruit of the Spirit—love, joy, peace, patience, kindness, goodness, faithfulness, gentleness, and self-control. But if we're speeding so quickly through our lives, it's hard to notice any of that richness or fullness, let alone make room for it or tap into it. When we're running full speed ahead, we don't feel like we can muster any patience or self-control, and we struggle to recall when we last felt anything resembling peace. We're zooming around so fast we don't have time to accept lovely invitations from God to connect with Him through prayer, reading our Bibles, being present, or celebrating the good stuff.

Accept lovely invitations from God to connect with Him.

But I want to.

Do you?

Are you ready to try? The pages ahead are packed with different ways Christians for centuries have been tapping into the full life Jesus promises. These ideas aren't new. And they're accessible for all of us. You don't need any money or experience or knowledge or privilege. You just need to be willing to make some room and slow down so you can catch a glimpse of the abundant life Jesus wants for you and invites you into.

PART 1

Rest

When a pipe burst in our kitchen while we were out of town, we ended up having to tear out all our kitchen cabinets and floors due to the extensive water damage. But before you can remove a cabinet or drawer, you have to empty it. And so, clearing out our entire kitchen became an immediate task I had to undertake.

I had no idea how much stuff I had crammed in cabinets and stashed on shelves until I started unloading them. How many times had I even used that cake pop maker? Garlic roaster? Candy dish that looked remarkably similar to another candy dish I owned? I like to buy cute paper plates and napkins for holidays or celebrations and usually end up using most but not all of a pack. And so there were three zoo animal plates, two Valentine's plates, and four dinosaur birthday plates with various napkins to match. Plus the shamrock and Lego napkins, and the ones in my kids' school colors. I could go on and on.

These kitchen items were taking up space in our home. But there are so many things that take up space in our lives—expectations, comparisons, the desire to get ahead, the fear of falling behind, distractions, old habits or relationships that no longer allow us to live in the fullness God has for us. We keep adding and stuffing them in another corner of our brain or calendar until, like my cabinets, we're crammed and jumbled with way more than we were ever intended to process, do, or handle. And as a result of trying to keep track of and be responsible for all the excess, we're exhausted, depleted, and run-down.

Does your life feel too full? Like you couldn't possibly add one more thing? Like you're tired or frazzled all the time? Jesus is giving you permission to rest. To put down some things. Clean house. Let go. He's inviting you to take a day off, take a nap, turn off your phone. He's encouraging you to breathe deeply and slowly.

We'll spend the first section of this book learning how to RSVP *yes* to God's glorious invitation to rest.

CHAPTER 1

On Running

Fast and Slow Rhythms

I'm a runner.

Actually, I *was* a runner until my left knee got mad at me a few years ago. Tightening up. Aching when I'd get out of a chair. Then it got downright angry. Buckling during a run, refusing to jog another step. I finally went to see an orthopedic doctor, hoping he could snap his fingers and let me run again. Apparently not.

The doctor sent me to get an MRI. The diagnosis was something about the cartilage in my knee rubbing against my kneecap. I landed in physical therapy, where I learned some exercises designed to prevent future injuries and my knee had time to rest and heal. Then I tentatively tried to run again. One mile one day. Two miles a few days later. And I learned through trial and error that I *can* run if

I take every other day off;
I stretch daily; and
I wear an ugly black knee brace when my knee feels wonky.

Now I'm a runner *and* a walker.

It took an injury to teach me to slow my pace.

I run a day and then walk a day, back and forth, run then walk, fast then slow, which sometimes makes me feel creaky. But it's what my body demands. I can't run two days in a row without consequences.

The same holds true for our lives: we can't run constantly without paying the price.

We can't run constantly without paying the price.

You and I were created to do and make things for God's kingdom. The apostle Paul said, "I urge you to live a life worthy of the calling you have received" (Ephesians 4:1). *The Message* version of that verse reads, "I want you to get out there and walk—*better yet, run!*—on the road God called you to travel" (emphasis added).

I get excited when I read that. I want to get out there and run. Do the things, meet the people, live out the calling God has put on my life, ask the questions, write the words. This instruction is good instruction.

But some days we need to walk.

Because we were also created to reduce our speed every now and then, to pause before and after all the places we're going and things we're doing. This isn't only for my knee. This applies to everything in our lives. My knee knows when I haven't taken time to slow down. Similarly, our souls know when we shortcut taking breaks in our schedules, when we ignore stillness. We get edgy and grumpy and exhausted. We feel the stress boiling up in us like a pot of pasta left on high too long. If we don't turn down the burner, we're going to boil over and make a mess of things.

Our culture calls us to be runners. To run every day in our work, relationships, volunteering, and commitments without resting or allowing time to stretch. The world encourages us to work a side hustle, be more productive, and achieve higher goals. And, yes, there is great work to be done. No question.

Still, Jesus frequently took time to get away from the crowds, from the busyness of His ministry, from His preaching, healings, and miracles (all excellent things), and He invites us to do the same. "Come to me, all you who are weary and burdened, and I will give you rest. Take my yoke upon you and learn from me, for I am gentle and humble in heart, and you will find rest for your souls. For my yoke is easy and my burden is light" (Matthew 11:28–30).

"Come to me, all you who are weary and burdened, and I will give you rest." (Matthew 11:28)

Are you weary? Are you burdened by anything?

Jesus offers rest.

Yes, God calls us from the very beginning of time to do good work (Genesis 1:28). But Jesus says His work? His yoke? It's easy. The work He calls us to isn't heavy or exhausting; it's light.

How can that be?

How can we do great things for God's kingdom, use the talents He's given us, pursue the passions He's put inside us, care for the people He's placed in our lives, and tend to all the urgent requests for our time and still end up rested?

Jesus tells us this can happen if we're willing to learn from His gentle and humble heart. From the rhythms of work and rest, go and slow, that He created and modeled. When we don't follow these rhythms, when we skip the slowing-down part of the cadence, we end up injured, depleted, anxious, or unable to do what God calls us to next. We also miss out on the beauty and refueling the stillness provides.

I look forward to my running days now more than ever, because I have a new appreciation for how precious they are. I put in my earbuds and go. I sweat out toxins from my body and mind as I pound my feet on the pavement or trail and process with God. I get my heart pumping and endorphins flowing, so grateful that I'm able to run. I cover more ground and I cover it faster than on walking days. I finish my workout with a sense of accomplishment, alert and focused.

But I've also come to look forward to the non-running days.

On walking days, I slow down. I notice the sunlight filtering through leaves. I breathe in and out. Walks are easier to schedule. I can walk a little in the morning and a little more after dinner. Often I'll recruit my husband, a friend, or one of our kids to join me. It's the perfect time to talk and share. That's harder on a run, because not all my people run, and the ones who do don't necessarily run the same mileage or pace as me. There's something therapeutic about the slow down, about talking while outside, surrounded by God's creation. About sharing lives shoulder to shoulder—in this together, moving forward.

And the stretching. Yikes! I feel it the next day if I don't pay enough attention to this step both before and after moving. If I'm trying to fit in a run before a meeting or return from a walk knowing it's time to start prepping dinner, it seems more convenient to skip the stretching or maybe zip through it. But those couple of minutes of intentional slowdown are game changers for how my body functions. Like taking a moment to pause and praise God for something grand that just happened or asking for His help before moving into the next conversation or task of the day. These cadences are so important—the slow and the go, back and forth, rest and work, sleep and wake, move and be still.

Jesus invites us, "Get away with me and you'll recover your life. I'll show you how to take a real rest. Walk with me and work with me—watch how I do it. Learn the unforced rhythms of grace" (Matthew 11:28–29 MSG).

Yes, please. Unforced rhythms of grace sound incredible.

We can have them if we want.

We get to choose.

To stay in the fast lane and try to do all the things on our own. To risk burnout or heartburn or burned-up resources, dollars, or relationships. *Or* to release the achievements, goals, and speed in which we get it all done to Jesus. Trusting that He knows what's best. That He *wants* what's best for you and me, His beloved children.

Our busy seasons of go, go, go can be exhilarating and productive. But they need to be balanced with relaxing afternoons and lingering dinners or a morning when we sleep in. We need the fast and the slow. It's the contrast that highlights the benefits of both.

Busyness beckons. We tend to ignore the stiffness in our souls, the aches in our hearts that are calling us to slow down. We keep going and going until we buckle. But we don't have to.

I like *the Message* paraphrase in Matthew 11, that Jesus says "walk with me," not "run with me." Jesus is on the move, but at a slower pace than the world might tell us we need to go. Which will you choose? The fast lane or the easy yoke?

Slow Down

> Come to me, all you who are weary and burdened,
> and I will give you rest. Take my yoke upon you and
> learn from me, for I am gentle and humble in heart,
> and you will find rest for your souls. For my yoke is
> easy and my burden is light. (Matthew 11:28–30)

In what areas of your life do you feel you're running too fast?

How does this idea of slowing down make you feel?

What's currently keeping you from slowing down your pace?

CHAPTER 2

Lighten Your Load
What Can You Let Go Of?

Knowing we need to slow down is one thing. Doing it? That's something else altogether.

I thought my friend Beth, who had just taken a four-day backpacking adventure on the Appalachian Trail, would have some stellar insights on slowing down. I mean, she'd signed up to be in the woods for four days. No car pools. No meetings. No cell service. So, shortly after her return I quizzed her about her excursion while we walked together on our favorite tree-lined trail.

I was looking for great tips on reducing the rapid pace of our lives. Instead, I learned a lesson on what needs to take place *before* we can slow down: lightening our loads.

"I could only carry thirty-two pounds in my backpack," Beth explained, gesturing excitedly. "It added up fast. That included clothes, breakfast, snacks, and water. I needed to consider *every* item I placed in my pack."

A blue jay squawked from a high-up branch as if to emphasize Beth's point.

Her comments made me think of Jesus's reference to a "light burden" in Matthew 11:30, and of what I'm carrying and how that's equipping or hindering me. Is my metaphoric backpack of life filled with things that are life-giving, necessary, and enjoyable? Or am I stuffing unhealthy relationships, extra to-dos, guilt, expectations, and even unnecessary possessions into my life and carrying them around, allowing them to weigh me down and deplete my energy? Was it perhaps time to clean out my pack?

How about yours?

Because here's the thing. If we're carrying too much, our burdens will never feel light.

If we're carrying too much, our burdens will never feel light.

We're bombarded with messages telling us we're supposed to keep adding things in. Have we made this recipe? Watched that show? Used this face cream under our normal face cream? Tried cold plunging? Everything we do—each lifestyle decision, thing we volunteer for, book we read, exercise we try—demands time and energy. They all take up space in our backpacks. If our pack has a finite amount of room, *and* we're trying to save space for times of rest and moments to be still with Jesus, then we need to sort out what stays and what goes.

How do we decide?

First, we need to take inventory of what all is jammed into our lives. What work do we do? What relationships are we in? When do we volunteer or help out? What are our responsibilities? How do we care for ourselves?

Evaluating what's in our packs can take time. But as we begin to become aware of how we're filling our days, we can start deciphering what matters and what is excess. We get to keep all the things that help us grow and thrive. We'll want to eliminate the things that don't.

We can ask ourselves, Is this necessary? How much time, money, or energy is this costing me? Does it interfere with something else? Is this relationship or activity draining or life-giving? If I had to give up one, which thing is more important? Less important? Does this bring me joy? Is that safe or healthy for me?

Those are all great questions for anyone. But if we're followers of Jesus, we can dig deeper. One way is by looking at how Jesus handled the temptation to jam His proverbial backpack with the bright and shiny things of this world.

In Luke 4 we find Jesus in the wilderness being tempted by the original tempter, Satan himself. First the devil tempts Jesus with bread. Turns out this isn't only about bread, although Jesus is famished. It's about if He trusts God to give Him what He needs.

Jesus answers Satan by quoting Deuteronomy 8:3, "Man does not live on bread alone but on every word that comes from the mouth of the LORD." I love that Jesus quotes Scripture to make His point. The devil talks about bread, trying to convince Jesus to fulfill His needs instead of trusting God to provide for Him.

We crave to be loved, to be seen, to matter.

Yes, Jesus was physically hungry. He'd been fasting for forty days! But we hunger for so many things. We crave to be loved, to be seen, to matter. And when we have that empty feeling inside, we're often triggered to "feed ourselves" with, yes, snacks but also substances, shopping, sit-ups, the new series everyone is talking about, social media—you name it. We turn to all the things the world tells us we "need," all the things the world tells us will make us happy and fulfilled. We try to fill our void with things we can see. Things we can grab. Things that feel like an instant fix. Instead of trusting God to provide for us.

Jesus always sees us, cheers for us, protects us, and believes that we matter.

The truth is, the only thing that will truly satisfy us, fill us with love and grace and purpose, is Jesus. His love for us never runs out or expires. It's Jesus who always sees us, cheers for us, protects us, and believes that we matter. It's Him and spending time in His Word that remind us of these truths. Everything else falls short, runs out, or gets replaced. We gobble up the things that Satan and the world try to distract us with only to get hungry again and again. Jesus promises, "Whoever comes to me will never go hungry, and whoever believes in me will never be thirsty" (John 6:35).

Something to think about before we stuff our backpacks or closets or calendars to fill a void.

Next, the devil shows Jesus "the kingdoms of the world" (Luke 4:5) and offers Jesus authority over them. Satan loves to dangle these same carrots in front of us.

You could be the CEO, Satan tempts.

You could get that guy's attention, the snake hisses.

You could be an influencer, get thousands of likes, the devil whispers.

Of course you can be a member of that exclusive club or live in that prestigious neighborhood or be included in that elite social group, the enemy offers.

But usually for a price.

To this temptation, Jesus responds, "Worship the Lord your God and serve him only" (v. 8).

Now, there is absolutely nothing wrong with being CEO, or being in a relationship or in a position of influence, or living in a certain neighborhood or belonging to a certain group, as long as Jesus is *more* important than these things. The problem comes when we start obsessing about climbing the ladder or earning the points or being seen and noticed. These things in themselves can be good things, great things even. But Jesus is better. He's the only one worthy of our worship. I want to remember this as I examine what I'm carrying.

Last but not least, Satan tempts Jesus to jump off the highest part of the enormous temple and summon angels to save Him. Jesus is God and could easily snap his fingers and call as many angels as it would take to stop or cushion His fall. But Jesus also knows God doesn't want us testing Him. Instead, God wants us to love Him, have a relationship with Him, trust Him, ask His opinion on what we should do next. So, Jesus responds, "Do not put the Lord your God to the test" (v. 12).

And Satan exits stage left.

God loves it when we call out to Him.

Let me clarify: God loves it when we call out to Him. He watches over and protects us (Psalm 121). But Satan wasn't asking Jesus to ask God for protection. The Enemy was suggesting that Jesus intentionally put Himself in danger and then test God to see what He would do. God would probably appreciate it if we stopped pushing the boundaries, stop putting ourselves in situations we know are dangerous for us. If we tend to spend too much money, why are we at the mall again or on the website that sells our favorite workout clothes? If we have a problem with alcohol, why do we keep a bottle of Chardonnay in our fridge? If we always get in an argument with that coworker over politics, why did we bring up the election over lunch? God can protect us, but why *invite* baggage into our lives that weighs us down?

So, let me ask myself and you again, What are we carrying? Because in order to live freely with Jesus, we need to lighten our loads.

In order to live freely with Jesus, we need to lighten our loads.

Jesus gave us a great starting point when He told the tempter what matters most in life:

1. The Word of God (aka the Bible, and Jesus)
2. Seeking God above worldly things
3. Trusting and obeying God

If we pack these essentials first, we'll still have room for so much more, because Jesus recognizes that we'll need more than those three things in our packs. Jesus ate, drank, paid taxes, went to weddings and dinner parties, traveled with friends, and taught crowds. Jesus spent quality time with His companions while working hard for the Father. He mediated the disciples' arguments and helped these twelve very different men live together despite their differences. Jesus empathizes with our full lives, with the balancing act of work, play, relationships, and responsibilities. He doesn't tell us we're not allowed to do these things; He just invites us to tuck spending time with God and trusting Him safely in our bags before we load them with anything else.

Jesus also modeled what not to carry. In His showdown with Satan, Jesus refused to make room for a reliance on material things, a hunger for power, or a tendency to stand too close to the edge.

Jesus asks us not to be fooled by the devil, advertising, our neighbor, best friend, or brother-in-law that we *need* to have season tickets, drink greens every morning, do CrossFit, take on more clients, or remodel our bathroom. We can do all those things, but if they become more important than our relationship with God, they will become heavy and burdensome.

The same week I walked with Beth, I also walked with my friend Juiquetta, who shared how God had been freeing her. "He's asked me to lay down some things I don't need to carry anymore," she told me, completely unprompted.

Two different friends. Two different days. Walking and talking about what we carry. Interesting.

As our feet crunched on fallen leaves, Juiquetta pulled a water bottle out of her snazzy leopard-print bag, took a sip, and commented, "I don't even know why I brought this bag. I could have held my keys in one hand and this water in the other. I am *always* trying to carry more than I need! Even this bag." She laughed.

Juiquetta's not the only one. I'm carrying too much. I'm guessing you might be too. This is our invitation to clean out those packs, make sure we have our essentials, pitch whatever has been weighing us down, and step into a freer life with Jesus—one that doesn't feel so heavy or crammed in, one with more room to hear and experience the goodness of God.

I don't want to fill up on empty promises or lies of what will fulfill me. Instead, I want to fill up on the Bread of Life that will always sustain me. You?

Slow Down

> Man does not live on bread alone but on every word that comes from the mouth of the LORD. (Deuteronomy 8:3)

Make a list of what you're carrying: the people you care for, the work you do, the tasks you're responsible for, how you fill your downtime, and so on.

Examine your list. Is anything more important to you than your time with God? Do you read the news without fail but struggle to find time to read the Bible? Do you never miss the latest episode or this week's game but go for days without praying? Do you work so many hours you haven't rested in . . . you don't know how long?

Pray over your list and ask God to help you. What is He asking you to empty out of your pack?

Write down two things you can do tomorrow to lighten your load. Some ideas: cancel an unnecessary meeting, set a time limit on your screen time, or reheat leftovers for dinner.

CHAPTER 3

You Can Have All This World

Avoiding Worldly Measures

It started so innocently.

My son had a role in the high school production of *Murder on the Orient Express*, and since it was December, I wanted to give him a train ornament as a memento on opening night. This was in the back of my brain while I was editing an article. The editing was tricky. And instead of plowing through it, I popped on Amazon for a "break." While browsing through multiple choices of trains, my brain wondered if my publisher had put up the "Read Sample" feature on the book I had releasing soon.

In the website's search bar, I typed the title. Then I scrolled down to the sales rank, even though the book hadn't come out yet.

Now I was down a rabbit hole. While I was down there, I kept burrowing in the dirt. I clicked on my author page and checked the sales ranking of my last two titles as well. It was a slippery slope I slid down. Leaving the work in front of me, searching for a little we're-proud-of-you gift for my son quickly morphed into a full-on distraction, with me trying to confirm my value as a writer based on one website. As if the number on the screen defined me in any way. Ick.

But it was a one-off. Right?

Wrong.

Because I proceeded to check these rankings for the next several days. Each time pulling away from the work at hand and assigning worth to myself based on the numbers I saw. I knew full well what I was doing. And still there I was, trying to justify myself as a writer.

I know. Why should I care? As if higher sales numbers in that split second of time made me a more legitimate writer, and lower sales rankings meant what? I wasn't a good writer? If I let my brain go there, it could spiral downward in a sticky mess of self-doubt and worry about my writing future (I'd been there before). But it would all be unfounded, because one snapshot of sales rankings isn't indicative of the big picture and certainly doesn't reflect God's call on my life.

Jesus calls me to write. To research books and write them honestly from my heart, from what He teaches me. And then He asks me to trust Him with the outcomes.

And I totally do.

Until I don't.

My husband is a professor and has something called Google Scholar where he can see how many times his scholarly articles have been cited by other researchers. My friend who runs a women's ministry monitors attendance at the events she plans. A big turnout equates to success. A small turnout means it's a failure. Maybe. But maybe not. Not if God brought the exact right people to the event and it changed their lives.

You might find your value in a number on a scale. Or how many people commented on that picture you posted—because your fam is super cute, right? Or how many orders you received, how fast you ran your race, how many goals you scored, what grade you got, how many people complimented the meal you made or the outfit you wore, how many zeros are on your paycheck, what your title is, how much weight you lifted, or how many volunteers signed up. These are all ways for us to keep score. And, yes, sometimes it's important for budgeting or strategizing or marketing or planning or monitoring to check numbers and results. But let's be honest: most of us check these things more than necessary. And we do it because we're seeking validation.

Oh look, I gained a pound (or lost one, depending on your goals)—woo-hoo! And then we weigh ourselves three more times that day. Five more people signed up for the event. And when we check an hour later, it's eight. Why haven't more folks registered in the last hour? I saved twelve dollars at the store. Wait, let me look at the receipt again, was it thirteen? Because I'm the best at finding bargains.

We waste time checking excessively. And each time we allow the world to tell us how good it thinks we are or are not. Which is part of living here on planet Earth.

But here's the issue. We live *in* this world, but we're not *of* this world (John 17:14–18). And also, Jesus doesn't keep score. I love how He handled a situation where the Pharisees were trying to pit Jesus and John the Baptist against each other by using a worldly metric. "Jesus realized that the Pharisees were keeping count of the baptisms that he and John performed (although his disciples, not Jesus, did the actual baptizing). They had posted the score that Jesus was ahead, turning him and John into rivals in the eyes of the people. So Jesus left the Judean countryside and went back to Galilee" (John 4:1–3 MSG).

Who leaves in the middle of winning the game? Jesus, that's who. Our Savior would have no part in this keeping score of baptisms.

This wasn't a one-off. This was how Jesus lived and modeled living for us. Later, when a group of Jewish people were questioning His authority, Jesus said, "And though I have no wish to glorify myself, God is going to glorify me. He is the true judge" (John 8:50 NLT).

Jesus didn't want to highlight Himself, or as Eugene Peterson paraphrases this verse, "I am not trying to get anything for myself" (MSG).

Really? Everyone else seems to be.

So much of our busyness is striving. It's sending one more email, posting one more thing, running one more drill, errand, or lap so we can earn another point on the scoreboard of life. So we can get the spotlight or a pat on the back for ourselves, our work, or our brand. And when we're feeling a little underqualified or underappreciated, we start grabbing for something, anything, that shouts, "You matter!"

But what if we didn't do this? What if instead of wasting precious moments of our days—moments we feel we don't have enough of—checking rankings, refreshing our email to see how many people responded, or comparing our numbers to his or hers, we used those moments to take a deep breath or ask God's advice? What if instead of filling our heads with worry about our metrics, we fully believed that God loves us? That He's already chosen us to be His—not because of our rankings or popularity or size or profits, but simply because He has.

He's already chosen us to be His—not because of our rankings or popularity or size or profits, but simply because He has.

Even before He made the world, God loved us and chose us in Christ to be "holy and without fault in his eyes" (Ephesians 1:4 NLT).

Let that truth sink in.

Jesus lived from a place of fully believing God loved Him and chose Him. When all that score keeping and comparison was going down in John 4, Jesus didn't waste one precious second engaging in an argument with the Pharisees. He didn't take the time to list all the prophecies of the Old Testament He fulfilled. He didn't remind them of the magi bringing Him royal gifts when He was born or the voice of God speaking over Him when He was baptized. He didn't flaunt the fact that His disciples had baptized more people than the Baptizer. Why bother? It was a waste of time. Instead, Jesus hid Himself from the crowd and slipped away.

What if we took justifying ourselves out of our backpacks? Cleared up that space in our minds and our spirits? Threw away that ugly feeling of trying to prove that we matter and lightened our loads?

Jesus was completely secure in His identity! The score was inconsequential to Him. The spotlight didn't matter. Jesus didn't crave it. He stepped away and sought time with God. Because when He hung out with God, God reminded Jesus that He was His beloved Son with whom He was pleased (Matthew 3:17; 17:5). God is telling us the same thing—we're His treasured children, and He's so pleased with us (Galatians 4:4–7). When we cling to that truth, we don't have anything to prove.

When the competition gets fierce, the pressure turns up, or insecurities loom, do we use our time to pull out old trophies, see who liked our posts, check our Amazon rankings? Do we make up conversations in our head about how we can validate ourselves to the world? Or do we take those moments to ask God to remind us of who we are and whose we are? Because there will *never* be a time when Jesus asks us to prove our worth to Him.

There will never *be a time when Jesus* asks us to prove our worth to Him.

"But you are a chosen people, a royal priesthood, a holy nation, God's special possession, that you may declare the praises of him who called you out of darkness into his wonderful light" (1 Peter 2:9). Get that? As God's people, we're chosen. We're royal. We're holy. We're God's special possession. Not because of our stats. Not because of any number associated with us. Not because of anything we've ever done. But because Jesus loves us.

Because Jesus loves *you*.

You heard my confession of my icky rankings checking. Every time I did it, I knew it was wrong, and yet I convinced myself it wasn't *too* wrong. It wasn't stealing or lying or killing someone. Still, I knew in my gut checking those numbers was a lack of trust in my identity in Christ.

Another crazy thing about checking those rankings is that it stole precious time away from me actually editing that article I was struggling with. We've been talking in this book about slowing down in the midst of all we need to do. And here I was wasting time on an unhealthy thing I had no need to do. It wasn't just the time on Amazon. It was the thinking about it later. It was the distraction and insecurity it created in my spirit. Talk about something that should come out of my backpack! What if instead I'd prayed for clarity for that article or allowed my thoughts to percolate? Gone for a quick walk down the street to spark creativity and get some fresh air? And how much more centered and peaceful would I have been if I hadn't given myself one more thing to worry about?

A few days into my Amazon searches, I attended a worship event and we were singing a modern take on the old hymn "Give Me Jesus." The refrain goes, "You can have all this world. Give me Jesus."

I was singing that refrain when I felt the Holy Spirit saying, "When you check your rankings for validation, you're acting like you want the world to judge you on its secular scale. If you really want Me, who loves you unconditionally, instead of the world and its metrics, you should stop."

This wasn't a demand from Jesus. He doesn't require us to never check worldly measurements. Sometimes they're necessary. But He is always inviting us into a more fulfilling life. And putting down our obsession with "how we're doing" in this world is one way we can better experience all the love and grace and peace He has for us.

In my heart I apologized for grabbing at things that don't truly define me, for thinking they could. For keeping score. I told Jesus I loved Him. I asked Him to help me remember that I am who He wants me to be no matter what any numbers say, and that He is everything I need.

Jesus is everything we need. He wants to fill us. He longs to satisfy us. He already loves us. Right now. Wherever we are. However we rank.

And as I sang, I was overwhelmed by His love.

The song has a line proclaiming that if I have Jesus, I don't need anything else. I sang it over and over, and each word sank in. I don't *need* rankings or reviews or sales numbers. I love to write for the Lord. But even if He said I had to stop, that would be okay as long as I still had Him.

Jesus is everything we need. He wants to fill us. He longs to satisfy us. He already loves us. Right now. Wherever we are. However we rank. He told a woman who had to draw water from a well every day: "Everyone who drinks this water will be thirsty again, but whoever drinks the water I give them will never thirst" (John 4:13–14).

Are you thirsty for attention, credit, value, confirmation, or proof of your worth? Jesus gave up His throne in heaven to live as a poor carpenter on this earth for you. He was ridiculed by the religious leaders even though He was God. He went through that for you. Jesus was betrayed by some of His best friends and endured a brutal, torturous death, all for you. That's how much value you have to Him.

Would we rather spend our time obsessing over the numbers and measurements of this world? Or living the life Jesus offers—the one that quenches our deepest thirsts? We get to choose.

Me? I already have everything I need and so much more. You can have all this world and the rankings and numbers associated with it. Give me Jesus.

Slow Down

> They had posted the score that Jesus was ahead, turning him and John into rivals in the eyes of the people. So Jesus left the Judean countryside and went back to Galilee. (John 4:3 MSG)

What worldly metrics feel like they define your worth or success?

How often or when do you tend to check these metrics?

Find "Give Me Jesus" on YouTube or Spotify, in a hymnal, wherever. It can either be the traditional African American spiritual or the 2021 version by UpperRoom. Listen to it. Maybe even sing along.

After listening, spend time praying about how you can intentionally steer clear from these worldly metrics.

CHAPTER 4

Less Hype and More Happy

Releasing Expectations

When my kids were little, I planned themed birthday parties. There was a pirate party where we bought an inflatable mini pool shaped like a pirate ship, complete with a puffy sail adorned with a smiley face and crossbones. It was on clearance at Walmart for eight bucks. We blew it up, filled it with water, and let the kids "set sail" in our front yard. I buried plastic gold coins in our sandbox before the party, and after their "voyage" we sent the kids on a treasure hunt.

There was also the Harry Potter party when my husband recorded himself as the voice of the Sorting Hat. We had each child sit in a chair and placed a big floppy hat on their heads and secretly pushed play. Then the hat (the recording of Brett) declared that each child should be in Hufflepuff or maybe Ravenclaw. My mom dressed up in a wizard costume she had from her days as an elementary school teacher, handed the kids Jelly Bellys, saying they were Bertie Bott's Every Flavour Beans, and asked them to guess what flavor they were. Grass or apple? These parties were as fun for me to plan as they were for my kids and their friends to experience.

But a couple of years ago when I asked my son what he wanted to do for his birthday, he asked, "Can we just invite my friends to Peffer Park and hang out and play in the creek and stuff?"

"Sure."

Long pause from me.

"If that's what you want."

Another deliberate pause.

"I'd be happy to take you all to see a movie. Or we could take your friends to the pool. That cool new waterslide is open."

"Is it okay if we go to the park?" my son asked in his kind, unassuming way.

"Of course."

It took Maguire asking me twice for me to truly hear that he didn't want something big or fancy. He just wanted simple.

Peffer Park consists of a grassy field with a shelter covering a few picnic tables, a bridge that spans a rocky creek, one swing set with four old-fashioned black U-shaped swings, and a firepit at the far end. Wooded trails head out from the actual park and are excellent for exploring. It's free. It's not fancy. But it's what my son wanted. So that's what we did.

As Maguire's friends arrived, they meandered toward the shelter and, without being asked, all set their phones on the picnic table. As if an invisible hand had hit a start button, all the boys took off toward the swings and jumped on them at the exact same time. Did I mention they were all entering their freshman year of high school?

After the swings, a couple more boys showed up, and they started a game of chase, then grabbed a football and tossed it around. Soon, they grabbed the water-squirter thingies my husband bought at the dollar store at the last minute because it was a scorching ninety-eight degrees. The boys soaked each other, laughing loudly. Before long they headed down to the creek. No agenda. No theme. We literally spent seven dollars on those water shooters plus a few bucks on bottled waters, hot dogs, buns, and s'mores supplies. That was it.

I did almost zero planning. Barely spent any time or money. And these kids were having the time of their lives.

I want to learn from these boys. To deprogram myself from thinking every event, coffee date, or dinner I host needs to look like Pinterest put the whole thing together. I want to enjoy nature and the people I'm hanging out with, then roast marshmallows until they are charred on the outside and gooey on the inside and slap them between two graham crackers with a chunk of chocolate and eat it up without caring that there is white sticky stuff all over my face because it tastes delicious—smoky and sweet, like summer camp.

What also brings me joy is one less thing—or twelve less things—on my list.

Don't get me wrong. I loved the planning and the execution of the kiddos' birthday celebrations when they were young. Figuring out snacks and crafts that would make them smile brought me joy. But what also brings me joy is one less thing—or twelve less things—on my list. Listening to my son and his friends laugh deeply. Less hype and more happy.

That birthday party made me wonder, What else am I making

too big a deal of? What other traps am I falling into of how things "need" to be or look? What else can I simplify?

I think of Jesus giving a crowd these instructions on living simply: "Therefore I tell you, do not worry about your life, what you will eat or drink; or about your body, what you will wear. Is not life more than food, and the body more than clothes? Look at the birds of the air; they do not sow or reap or store away in barns, and yet your heavenly Father feeds them. Are you not much more valuable than they? Can any one of you by worrying add a single hour to your life?" (Matthew 6:25–27).

I love verse 26 of this passage in *The Message* version: "Look at the birds, free and unfettered, not tied down to a job description, careless in the care of God. And you count far more to him than birds."

Free. Unfettered. Not tied down. I'd love to feel that way all the time. I've lived long enough to know unfettered isn't always possible. We have responsibilities. We have obligations. Everything from "I need to fill out four forms, get my blood drawn, and have a minimum of three doctor appointments each year if I want to maintain my current health insurance discount" to "Somebody *has* to clean the toilets in our house." I'm tied down to those responsibilities. However, there are so many other things—too many other things—in my life that *I* tie myself down to, like feeling the need to plan elaborate birthday parties. This is something I can let go of.

One assignment I gave myself was blogging weekly. At the beginning of my writing career, I was told how important it is to consistently create and deliver content. That made sense. But a few years back my publicist suggested I reduce my blogging to every other week. Really? What was she speaking of? Ever since I started blogging, I'd never looked back. It was a way to write consistently and get the good news of Jesus out there. Cutting back felt strange, foreign, like I was cheating or slacking somehow. But when my publicist said this, I heard the soundtrack from *Hamilton* playing in my head, asking me, "Why do you blog like you're running out of time?"

The weekly blog worked when I was starting out, and again for a season when I didn't have any book contracts. But it wasn't working in this season. And I was allowed to let go of that. Blogging half as often freed up hours to focus on the books I was under contract to write. When I realized the relief in giving myself permission to slow down, I wanted to open my hands and calendar and home and let Jesus remove any other arbitrary assignments I'd given myself that were stealing time and freedom from my life.

Reflecting on the expectations we put on ourselves and if they're necessary or not is helpful, but we also need to make sure we're not heaping the expectations others put on themselves on ourselves.

One of my friends vacuums her home every day. Another's Christmas decorations look like the set of a Hallmark movie. My mom's garden is always blooming. Even in the winter in Ohio she has ornamental cabbages decorating her lawn. None of these things are wrong or bad. It would be lovely if someone vacuumed my house daily. My friend's home looks spectacular during the holidays, and my mom's flower beds are gorgeous.

But if I felt I "needed" to do all these things because my friends and mom do, I'd have zero time to breathe or shower or sleep. I can do some of these things—but I have to give myself grace and loosen my grip on the "need" to do what the people around me do, on letting comparison dictate how I spend my time. My house needs vacuumed. But not every day. My friend who does this has two giant dogs. We have zero pets. Sometimes it will go over a week before I vacuum. And that's okay. I plant a few hearty flowers in the spring because I really do love flowers. I try to remember to water them, but I don't always. Some of them shrivel and die every year. And I'm all right with that. Because if I had an extra half an hour a day, gardening isn't how I would choose to use it.

I love all things Christmas, especially lights. But outdoor lights are something I delegate to our big kids. I don't understand how to make them stick to the house or plug in somewhere. I would rather focus my holiday prep time on baking and decking the indoor halls. I'm not being lazy when I do these things; I'm letting go of some unnecessary pressures and false expectations.

How about you? Anything you feel you need to do a certain way, to a certain degree, but you're not even sure why you have that expectation?

If we let go of some of these false perceptions of how we need to live, our lives would feel less fettered.

If we let go of some of these false perceptions of how we need to live, our lives would feel less fettered. We have permission to release them. Jesus never told us we have to throw Pinterest-worthy parties or cook like we're on the Food Network or have homes that look like Jojo decorated them. He never said we have to look like her or him. Just because that person next to us picked up their phone to tackle some of their email doesn't mean we're falling behind if we don't. We have permission to keep our phone in a resting position and simply breathe.

We have permission to keep our phone in a resting position and simply breathe.

What are you insisting you do that is inhibiting you from the liberating life Jesus offers?

I'm picturing those teenage boys on the swings, free as birds in the air. They weren't worried about what they were wearing, what anyone thought of them, who might or might not message them, or what time it was. They were simply savoring life. And it was beautiful.

I want to be more like those boys. "Careless in the care of God" (Matthew 6:26 MSG). Remembering that God has me, loves me, wants good for me. And if the laundry hamper overflows or I don't finish reading the book before small group, it's okay.

God still loves us. He still wants what's good for us. That doesn't change. Ever. I'd like to trade in some of my arbitrary expectations for a good back-and-forth on a swing, my toes reaching to the bright blue of the sky and hair blowing in my face.

Hop on. The swing next to me is open.

Slow Down

> Look at the birds, free and unfettered, not tied down
> to a job description, careless in the care of God. And
> you count far more to him than birds. (Matthew
> 6:26 MSG)

Over the next few days, take note of some ways you might be putting too much pressure on yourself.

Decide to let go of something—a ritual, false obligation, or task you assign yourself. Ask Jesus to give you ideas of what you can release.

Journal about how it makes you feel to let go of things, and about how you felt after letting go of that specific thing.

If releasing that thing brought you freedom, decide to release it again next week or month. If it ended up not bringing you freedom, try something else.

CHAPTER 5

Il Giorno di Riposo
Sabbath

My workweeks are wacky. I'm a self-employed creative. I choose my work schedule, so I try to maneuver it around my family's routines. I also have nonwork tasks like doing laundry, getting groceries, sending out emails for the soccer team fundraiser I agreed to chair, and ordering new khakis for my youngest, because the ones he tried to wear to school today were so short it looked like he'd been chatting with Noah and was expecting a flood. And because I have multiple responsibilities, sometimes my vocational work spills into the evenings while we're watching an episode of *The Great British Baking Show* or while the kids are doing homework because, well, there's a lot to do.

I'm not the only one. In the past two weeks I've been blessed to visit with four different friends. Each coffee date or walk took weeks (or months) of back-and-forth texting to find a time that worked for both me and my friend because—you guessed it—our schedules are so full. One friend confided that her volunteering had started to get in the way of her other volunteering. Another said she hadn't had time to move her body and get any exercise in weeks. A third told me she was trying to make sure her daughter who was struggling was taken care of before she took care of herself. These women are all incredible. They love their families and friends well. They do important work—some they get paid for and some they do not. They are smart and passionate and also exhausted.

Maybe you don't have a zillion to-dos. But you're depleted because of a mental or physical ailment that makes it challenging to get out of bed. You're worn out. Or maybe it's not your ailment, but you spend your time and energy caring for someone you love. Your workload of caring for yourself or another is exhausting you.

God works too. He's constantly pumping air into our lungs, turning the lights on in the sky, and watering the grass. He's healing relationships, giving us peace and courage, and doing so very much more. But God, who invented the world and work and us, didn't intend for us to burn the candle at both ends.

God, who invented the world and work and us, didn't intend for us to burn the candle at both ends.

At the beginning of the world, God created the entire earth, then on the sixth day He created land animals, then people, and told the people to take care of the earth. To govern it. To reign over it (Genesis 1:28). That's an extremely large project.

"The LORD God took the man and put him in the Garden of Eden to work it and take care of it" (2:15). Fruit needed picked. Seeds needed gathered and sown. Plants needed water. But it was beautiful work. And God, being God, had already decided the perfect way to make this work fulfilling, not exhausting.

By inventing rest.

It was the very next thing God did after creation. "By the seventh day God had finished the work he had been doing; so on the seventh day he rested from all his work. Then God blessed the seventh day and made it holy, because on it he rested from all the work of creating that he had done" (vv. 2–3).

This resting-on-the-seventh-day idea wasn't just for Adam and Eve. When God handed out the Ten Commandments to Moses, rest was number four on His top ten list. "Remember the Sabbath day by keeping it holy. Six days you shall labor and do all your work, but the seventh day is a sabbath to the LORD your God. On it you shall not do any work. . . . For in six days the LORD made the heavens and the earth, the sea, and all that is in them, but he rested on the seventh day. Therefore the LORD blessed the Sabbath day and made it holy" (Exodus 20:8–11).

It was how God set up the work-rest rhythm on day seven of the existence of the world. But the Israelites had been enslaved for 430 years (12:40), and during their slavery, it's doubtful they had any days off. God is telling His children, "Hey, I know Sabbath wasn't a thing when you were slaves, but you're no longer slaves. You now have the freedom and privilege and ability to get into my perfect rhythms of grace—ones where you work and rest. In fact, you get an entire day to lay down your burdens and recover every single week. I'm giving you the gift of rest back. Take advantage of this gift."

Who wouldn't? I mean, who doesn't want a day off?

Apparently we don't.

Because we're still working like maniacs, threadbare. I'm struggling to connect with dear friends because our to-do lists are too long and our planners too packed.

How is it possible to slow down? A neighbor needs a hand. Our little gets sick. Our supervisor asks us to come in on our day off. The committee chair asks for a few minutes of our time that turns into an hour or two or three. Our loved one has an emergency. Our work is charity or ministry, and the more of it we do, the more people are helped. There's simply so much we want and need to do, and so we feel the need to complete some of it during nonwork hours. And if you're a mom or caretaker, there are no nonwork hours.

Maybe no one demands that we work every waking moment, but we know if we called one more client or read one more book with our kiddos or volunteered one extra shift, we'd feel more productive, get a little ahead, help someone else get ahead, or make some extra cash. Sometimes we feel guilty when we put the work down, because shouldn't we be doing one more thing?

God invites us into downtime.

But God invites us into downtime. Because our loving heavenly Father knows we need it. Our bodies aren't designed to go 24-7. Mine tells me when I go too hard. I get grumpy and get headaches. I bet your body and brain signal when you're overworked or overstressed too. God craves for us to be able to face Monday not "needing" #mondaymotivation or an extra shot of espresso to get us going, but ready to dive in headfirst, excited to do the good work He calls us to, refreshed and refueled by Him.

God also gave us Sabbath so we can reflect on the work we did the previous six days. God modeled this for us. After everything God created at the beginning of time, God paused and said, "Mm-hmm, that sky and water, they are good. Those fish with their scales—what a cool idea I had. And feathers for the birds? Simply brilliant. I made it so they can fly!" Then on the seventh day, when "the heavens and earth were completed in all their vast array" (Genesis 2:1), God blessed that seventh day and made it a holy day.

What work did you do this past week? Have you looked over it? Reflected on how it went? If you're a real estate agent, did you help someone find a new home? Wow! If you're in recovery, did you attend rehab? Make a small step forward? Way to go! If you're a teacher, did you take time to celebrate that beautiful moment when the student who's been struggling read that sentence? Out loud? To the entire class? Amazing! If you're a nail tech, did you sit back to admire the manicure you gave to the woman headed to a wedding? So pretty! If you volunteer at the hospital, did you savor that special conversation with the new patient? You put them at ease! If you're a grandparent, have you taken time to really look at the sweet drawings you and your grandkids did together? Priceless!

And when you consider the work you did this past week, do you remember to thank God for His major role in those good works?

If we never pause, when do we reflect?

It's important to step back and thank God for all He does—for connecting those dots; giving us the idea, energy, clarity, or words; bringing that person's voice forward; managing that potentially volatile moment. If we never pause, when do we reflect? How do we evaluate what we should do next? How do we know what we should drop and what we should pick up? When do we appreciate that some of the work was truly good and praise God for it?

Of course, our work isn't finished on day six. Our work will never be finished. There will always be more kingdom work to do and more ways to shine Christ's light. But Sabbath isn't about being done. God didn't stop working once the world was created. He's still on the move every day, answering prayers, healing bodies, saving souls, giving us instruction, hope, guidance, courage, peace, and love. Sabbath isn't about crossing the finish line. It's about realigning ourselves, being grateful for the work we got to do with God, and trusting Him with whatever is next.

My Italian friend Andrea was explaining to me that the Italian verb *posare* means to put things where they go, to place them in their correct spots. Like when we put away dishes in the correct cupboards. The verb *riposare* comes from that same verb—to "re-posare." But *riposare* isn't used when putting things back in their place, like clean forks in the silverware drawer. Instead, it's used to speak of rest—that in resting, we are resetting things to how they should be. In fact, Italians call Sabbath *il giorno di riposo*, literally "the day of resetting" to put our lives back to how they should be.

I love that so much. A day to put things back to how they should be.

God can accomplish whatever He wants while we're resting.

Part of the beauty of Sabbath is remembering that, sure, we showed up this week, but everything we achieved only happened because God made it so. Which means God can also accomplish whatever He wants while we're resting. Sabbath is a way to say, "God, my work is yours. Please take care of what you want to take care of. Everything won't fall apart if I rest, because you're the one actually holding things together, not me." Sabbath forces us to cease our striving and to admit our dependance on the one true God. And there is such relief in knowing the weight of the world is *not* on our shoulders.

Growing up I heard the word *Sabbath* and thought it meant going to church on Sundays. Which is grand. But there is so much more available to us through this weekly rest. Sabbath is an invitation to find enjoyment and peace. To build our trust muscles, rely on God more and ourselves less. To detox from things we think we need but actually don't. Sabbath is a gift God created from the beginning. But most of the world has forgotten about Sabbath again. We're no longer slaves to Pharaoh but to the constant pinging of our phones, performance, and the perception that if we slow down or stop at all, we'll miss out.

The opposite is actually true. When we slow down, we catch our breath and discover that rest is a gift. When I first understood Sabbath this way, I was challenged. I wanted that rest but had no idea how I could find it. In our culture? Where Sundays are filled with basketball games and homework for the kids? Where everyone still needs to eat and errands need to be run? I had to think and pray through how that could work, how I might reorganize my time and tasks to make it happen. I brainstormed what could be restful and what I could lay down.

I talked to my husband about what I hoped to do, how it would affect our routines, and I invited him to join me. I started slow—a few hours off each weekend. I set some boundaries. And it's taken off from there. It's gone from being a partial-day experiment to a full day I look forward to each week.

Sunday is my Sabbath—the day I close my laptop and shut the door to my writing nook. I don't turn on my phone until noon and refrain from social media all day. I'm less distracted and more present. My husband and I usually go for a walk and treat ourselves at our favorite local coffee shop, where Brett gets a caramel cortado and I get a mocha with macadamia milk, before we grab the teenagers and head to church. I sometimes take naps on Sundays and usually find time to sit down with my journal and a good book. I may or may not cook depending on if that sounds delightful or not. Kneading pizza dough or simmering a soup is usually therapeutic for me, but if it sounds like something else to add to the to-do list, we might eat leftovers or order pizza.

When our kids were little, I didn't take Sabbath. Reflecting back, I don't know how I would have made it work. But I know that I could have. That Jesus would have helped me figure it out if I had asked Him. That wouldn't have meant I wasn't a mom on those days, just that I would have rested from some of my responsibilities. I would've still needed to change diapers and nurse the baby and give baths. But I could have been easier on myself, setting up our schedule so I could exhale more.

Some weeks I can't Sabbath on Sundays, so I do it another day that week. God's completely fine with that. He's not holding us to a certain day. It's just helpful to have a set day so we can stay consistent and keep that lovely rhythm of working six days and resting one.

I have friends who don't cook or do any shopping or cleaning on their Sabbaths, because in their hearts they know those tasks preoccupy them and kick them into an achievement mentality. Refraining from these tasks one day a week clears their minds and lifts a burden from their souls. I have a friend who runs every day, but on her Sabbath she walks, letting her body have a break from the work it does. Our older son leads worship, so most of his Sundays are spent rehearsing and leading others to Jesus through song. Sundays are life-giving to him, but they're not restful. He's also in college, so each semester he chooses a day when he doesn't have class for his Sabbath.

Sabbath is one of God's presents to us—a chance to rest, exhale, reflect, and recharge.

You'll have to figure out what works best for you. We're not supposed to overanalyze if we're doing Sabbath "right" or not. It's not mandatory. It's a gift. This is one of God's presents to us—a chance to rest, exhale, reflect, and recharge. The Lord told Moses in Exodus 16:29, "They must realize that the Sabbath is the LORD's gift to you" (NLT).

If we clear our calendars of work on our Sabbaths, then how do we spend our time? Doing something restful. Something that connects us to Jesus.

One approach is if you work with your mind, then Sabbath with your hands. And if you work with your hands, then Sabbath with your mind. If you're a gardener or painter, puzzles and books could be lovely ways for you to Sabbath. Since I'm a writer, snipping flowers from my yard to put in Mason jars or baking cookies loaded with semi-sweet chocolate chips provides me with rest.

As I started not only laying down work but also picking up peaceful things, I began enjoying Sabbath more and more, looking forward to it each week as a mental break for me. Sabbath is now refreshing. Renewing. A gorgeous treat. I now wake up

Monday mornings more clearheaded, focused, ready, motivated, and energized to do the work in front of me.

I savor my Sabbaths. You can too.

Slow Down

> They must realize that the Sabbath is the Lord's gift
> to you. (Exodus 16:29 NLT)

Do you take a weekly Sabbath? If so, what does it look like? Are there any ways you could make it more restorative?

If not, start this week. Choose a day when you can lay down your work. Can't imagine taking off a full day? No problem. Start slow. Set aside a morning or afternoon or at least a couple of hours. Talk to Jesus about what He wants you to rest from that day. Plan something relaxing for that time—a nap, a good meal, quality time with someone you adore.

Put it in your calendar again for next week.

CHAPTER 6

The Art of Saying No
Consider Your Commitments

Never say no to a book deal.

It's one of those soundtracks most writers have playing in the back of their minds. That doesn't mean writers should take opportunities that are trashy, conflict with their beliefs, or exploit their talents. But it does emphasize the truth that book deals are small miracles. The popular statistic is that only 1 to 2 percent of all manuscripts submitted to publishers get published.[1] Needless to say, when a book offer comes your way, you should have your eyes open and your yes ready.

I'm guessing you have a similar soundtrack in your life. Maybe it sounds like, "You should never say no to travel, a dinner invitation, a donation, a new client or patient, or a chance to see your grandbabies." These rules of thumb make sense *most* of the time.

Last week, I got the green light from my publisher to write this very book you're reading, along with another one I'd proposed. I literally dropped to my knees to praise God, then darted down the stairs from my writing nook to my husband's office and told him the amazing news. My family celebrated with me, because two books is a huge, huge deal! And celebrating is so important (check out chapter 22, "Cymbals and Drumsticks").

Then I unexpectedly got an invitation from an editor friend to write a third book.

It's unheard of to get three book deals in a week. All this book abundance was from Jesus. I'm still overwhelmed by His provision as I type this.

And then the craziest thing happened.

I got an email from yet another editor, inviting me to write yet another book for the Christian imprint she manages. I was speechless. I sent a message to my agent: "What in the actual world is going on?"

I was excited about yet another opportunity, another book deal. I was flattered and grateful. I was also worried about how I would meet all the deadlines. How frantic my life would be if I accepted. I'd had a dry spell in my writing before—a four-year period without any books. And honestly, remembering that time made me hesitant to turn a book down. I started praying. I asked my family and my agent to pray with me for discernment.

I told God, "If you want me to write this fourth book for you, I absolutely will. But if you don't, if this isn't how you want me to use my time, please show me, because then I don't want to do it. Please make it clear what you want me to do. Amen."

A myriad of thoughts went through my mind, including the soundtrack I mentioned earlier: *never say no to a book deal*.

I also wondered if I could really give each manuscript my best. If I accepted this fourth book, my workload, and therefore my life, would get extremely hectic while writing this book titled *The Urgency of Slowing Down*. Something about that felt very wrong.

On a walk with my husband to talk through the pros and cons, Brett mentioned the manna God provided for the Israelites while they were in the desert. "Then the LORD said to Moses, 'I will rain down bread from heaven for you. The people are to go out each day and gather enough for that day. In this way I will test them and see whether they will follow my instructions. On the sixth day they are to prepare what they bring in, and that is to be twice as much as they gather on the other days'" (Exodus 16:4–5).

I could see how all these book deals were like manna. It felt like God had literally rained these opportunities down from heaven for me. Still, I was operating out of a bit of a scarcity mentality—afraid of what would happen if I turned down a book deal.

In this passage from Exodus, we see that as God promised, the next morning the ground was covered with bread they called manna (v. 15). They got out jars and gathered the manna, and everyone had exactly what they needed. Amazing! Our God is such a perfect provider.

Our God is such a perfect provider.

As Brett and I chatted about this miracle in the Bible, he reminded me of what happened next—when the Israelites worried if God would give them bread the next day, even though He'd promised He would.

> Then Moses said to them, "No one is to keep any of it until morning."
> However, some of them paid no attention to Moses; they kept part of it until morning, but it was full of maggots and began to smell. (vv. 19–20)

"Maybe you're not supposed to stash any manna in a 'jar,' worried about if there will be more," Brett said. "Maybe instead you're supposed to take what you need and trust God to provide more when it's time."

This was the tension. A tension so many of us feel: If we don't take it, we'll miss out. If we don't go to that gathering, will we fall out of the social circle? If we don't lead the spring Bible study, will we ever be asked to lead another one? If we don't attend that conference, will we fall behind in our industry? If we don't join that board, will we be missing out on opportunities?

None of these things are bad things to do. But if we take on things that stress us out or compromise our relationships or physical or mental health, if our hearts are doing them so we don't miss out or because we don't believe God will provide, they can be like that smelly, maggoty manna—not good at all. Yucky and distasteful.

Eww! I definitely didn't want my writing to be "full of maggots." Or to smell. And yet, that soundtrack still played in the background of my brain like bad elevator music: *never say no to a book deal.* I'm guessing the Israelites were listening to a similar soundtrack. They were hungry. They'd been enslaved. Now they were roaming the desert. They'd probably been told, "Never turn away a good meal," or "If you see food, grab it. You never know when you'll find food again, especially in a desert." And so, the Israelites hoarded the manna, even though God promised to send it daily. And when they hoarded it, it rotted.

What is culture telling you that you should always say yes to? Because yeses are great . . . until we have too many of them. "Never turn down a glass of champagne" sounds fun, until you accept too many and get the headache that accompanies them. "Never turn down free tickets to a show" sounds great, until you find yourself going to see shows you don't enjoy, or your weekends are so booked that you don't have any downtime, or you're spending a fortune on parking, pre-show dinners, and babysitters that make those tickets far from free. "Always volunteer when the church asks." That one sounds noble—unless you're volunteering at church so much that you're neglecting your family, or you feel burned-out.

Our yeses and noes hold weight. It's important to examine why we're saying yes and no to things. Because they sound fun? Make us feel special or powerful? Make us look good? Because we want to help *everybody*? We're afraid we won't have another chance? We don't believe God could find someone else to do the job? Because we don't believe God is big enough to make things work out some other way?

How are you at saying no?

As I looked at what was already on my plate, adding a fourth book project sounded possible with lots of late nights and early mornings. But it also sounded super stressful. This was in November, and I wanted to savor Thanksgiving and Christmas with our family. I wanted to bake cookies and sit around a cozy, crackling fire, sharing stories without feeling a tug from my laptop. I had a getaway scheduled with my husband in February. I didn't want to be preoccupied with the fact that this fourth book opportunity was due in February (before all the others) and be distracted while walking on the beach with Brett, not slowing down enough to notice the calming sound of the waves or the warmth of his hand in mine.

We're not capable of or intended to do all the things all the time or to say yes to everything.

63

I'm sure you have opportunities coming your way as well. Could you chair this committee? Bring the snack? Speak at our next meeting? Help us set up? Be the team mom? Some of those things you should definitely say yes to. You are the perfect person for the job. But we're not capable of or intended to do *all* the things *all* the time or to say yes to *everything*. God will provide opportunities for us. So we don't have to hoard them.

Jesus knew this. He chose His yeses and noes deliberately. Jesus aligned His choices with the Father's will for Him in that moment. Not with His own preferences. Not with what the crowd, or His friends, or the religious leaders thought He should do or expected Him to do. Not with what might be perfect for someone else or even for Him at a different time. But always with what the Father wanted Him to do. Jesus said yes to things like letting the children come to Him (Matthew 19:14) and talking to a Samaritan woman, which was culturally unacceptable (John 4:7–9, 27). Both of these things surprised His disciples.

Jesus also said no to things.

Jesus also said no to things. He told Peter, "No, don't use that sword. Put it away." Jesus's disciples must have been shocked that He didn't want them to use violence or resistance—that He was going to willingly go with the soldiers who came to arrest Him (John 18:10–11). But in all these instances, Jesus was being obedient to God's will—loving His people well and even willingly walking to the cross so He could save you and me.

What are you being asked to do right now? Does someone want

you to be a mentor or a chaperone, or to plan the reunion? Some of these things are good things, some of them are great things, but only a very small number of them are the *best* things for you today. God gave you time. And it is precious. If we're going to slow down, we need to lighten our loads, not only of possessions and time on our phones but also of commitments. We can't pile every opportunity that comes our way onto our stacks. We want to leave room for resting rhythms.

God gave you time. And it is precious.

What if when God asks us to, we step away? One less meal we bring. One less shift we take. One less seminar we attend. One less party we plan. And we take that time away—the half hour, or week, or season—and use it to find alone time with God and ask Him, "What's next?"

How do you know when you should say yes or no?

Before you automatically answer an ask, offer, or invitation, politely tell the person, "That's such a lovely offer." Or, "Wow, I'm flattered you would ask." Or, "I love the work that group is doing." And then say, "Could I have a few days to pray about it and get back to you?" Anyone who gets angry or doesn't give you time is not being respectful of you or your boundaries. Some folks will be surprised or even put off, but most will agree that, of course, you can have time to pray over the decision. Then it's your job to actually pray.

Ask Jesus what the most important things He's asking you to do are. Ask Him how to make time for those things. Ask Him if there's enough room in your schedule to add anything in.

Ask Jesus if it's His will for you to do it. Or not. Ask Him to show you if there's any specific reason you should or shouldn't do this.

Reading our Bibles regularly can also help us process what to say yes and no to.

I already told you how my husband brought up the passage about manna and maggots. Additionally, over that weekend, our small group read Genesis 22, which is a passage all about God's promise to provide a son for Abraham—how the Lord will provide. I felt God reminding me that He was capable of providing additional book deals in the future, if that was His will. That I didn't have to say yes to all of them.

Another helpful tool for discernment is talking over your decision with people whose faith and opinions you value. I recruited my agent and family to pray for me. Good Christian community can help us discern God's will. My agent suggested I wait until Monday to respond to the editor, allowing me time to pray and think through things. On Saturday I had that manna conversation with my husband, and on Sunday I read Genesis 22. My agent's wisdom set me up to hear what the Bible said. The people I invited into my decision collectively pointed me back to who God is and what His will was.

Is there anything God is asking you to say no to?

Is there anything God is asking you to say no to? To give up? To pass on? To let go of?

We can't say no to everything that feels hard or inconvenient or time-consuming. We have responsibilities. And Jesus calls us to be His hands and feet, to help others in need. But we *can* proactively seek God's will when we're asked to do something new. We can pause. Pray. Turn to the Bible. Seek wise counsel. And see what God has to say.

Some decisions are no-brainers based on how God created us and what our current life looks like. Is that a strength of ours? Would we be a horrible fit? Is it during a time slot we even have available? Which of the options makes the most sense? Is this the thing we've been waiting for, praying for? Is there another way we can help?

With some opportunities, we've been asked about them so many times we know by now what our responses should be. What happened when we said yes in the past? What happened when we said no? Do we have any reason to believe it will be different this time? Better? Worse?

Lots of wonderful, interesting prospects will come our way, like manna from heaven. But we're not supposed to hoard them. We're supposed to trust God. He is a God of abundance.

I emailed the editor, thanked her profusely for the opportunity, and declined that extra unexpected book deal.

Next week, month, season, or year, God might call me to accept a project that comes out of the blue when I have other responsibilities. Or He might ask me to turn down more and more things. How will I know?

I'll have to stay in my Bible, keep praying, and invite special, trusted people into my prayerful discernment. If I do that, I'm confident God will make it clear.

How about you? Let's take charge of our schedules by seeking God's counsel on when to say yes and when to say no, no matter what we think we should do based on culture or habit or what we've been told.

Slow Down

> Then Moses said to them, "No one is to keep any of
> it until morning."
>
> However, some of them paid no attention to Moses;
> they kept part of it until morning, but it was full of
> maggots and began to smell. (Exodus 16:19–20)

Pull out your calendar for next week. Pray over it, asking God
to show you what's most important, what you could say no to.

Have you been asked to take on any new responsibilities lately?
Try this process before you decide what you'll do:

1. Pray
2. Read your Bible daily
3. Recruit trusted community into your prayerful decision-making

CHAPTER 7

How Much Is Enough?

Decluttering

I once knew a man who became so concerned with what he had that he lost sight of who he was. He started stealing money from his clients—just a little.

Then a little more.

And then even more.

Because when he did, he could get more things. The man believed the lie that these things defined him. All along, the fact that Jesus created him and loved him was where this man's immeasurable worth came from. It's where each and every one of us gets our worth from. But the man couldn't see it. He was blinded by more. He started buying paintings by famous artists and designer shoes and gold watches, finer things than he'd ever owned. It got to the point where he had so much art that he needed to rent a storage unit to keep what he didn't have room to display on his walls. He started stashing extra pairs of Italian loafers and Rolex watches at his office because there wasn't room for all of them in his closet at home. Sound crazy? It is, actually. But it's also true.

Eventually, the man got caught by his firm, was asked to leave his job, and had to remove himself altogether from his profession.

You're probably not guilty of white-collar crime, but I fear we all believe from time to time that if we had more, we'd be more. Jesus never says that. But the world does. On repeat. Most of us probably don't have an extra stash of designer shoes, but we probably have a pair of shoes (or two or more) that we haven't worn in over a year.

I learned the art of being thrifty at an early age. My parents grew up poor and got married and pregnant with my brother while still in college. I came along as my dad finished law school. They had to skimp and save to get by. If there was one ravioli left over from dinner, you put plastic wrap on it and put it in the fridge because someone might eat it. If your paper napkin from lunch wasn't messy, you folded it and reused it at your next meal. You bought coats in the summer and swimsuits in the winter because they were on clearance.

These lessons helped me straight out of college when I interned for free at an advertising firm by day while waitressing at night to make rent. This instinct to save anything I might use later and stock up on items on sale served me well again when my husband and I had our third and fourth babies. We were living on next to nothing while I stayed home with the littles, and he worked toward his PhD. During that season, I loaded up weekly on the unlimited supply of free books and movies from the library to entertain the kids. I learned that a pot of pasta feeds a whole family for only a couple of dollars, and if there's a free sample of something, you should probably take it.

Those are good lessons to learn. But somewhere along with all the saving, I also started holding on to things a little too tightly. What if we could use the rest of that construction paper for another craft? What if I could wear that bridesmaid dress again sometime? My intentions came from a great place, from a desire to reuse and save money and not be wasteful. And who knows, maybe someone would wear that crazy clown wig for a costume party in the future.

Maybe. But maybe not.

Maybe some of those things I was holding on to were just cluttering our home and my headspace. Maybe all those old VeggieTales DVDs, although hilarious and awesome, would now better serve a young family. Our youngest is seventeen! And if we gave those DVDs away, it would be easier to find the *National Treasure* DVD our family watches over and over, even though we stream most everything else. I'd also have room to keep a blanket in the entertainment center, so I wouldn't have to run upstairs and grab one every time someone wanted to get cozy on the couch.

How about those puppets? The board games no one has played in years? Maybe when I hold on to stuff, I'm acting a little like that man I once knew. Like I don't believe God will provide everything I need, that I need to hold on to all the options just in case, that things bring me some sort of security or purpose.

Over one third of United States garages are so full that homeowners can't park in them.

I'm not the only one. According to a study by Craftsman tools, over one third of United States garages are so full that homeowners

71

can't park in them.[1] What are we doing with all this stuff? Why are we holding on to it?

God has been doing a number on me about what I actually need. And about what He provides. God provided water from a rock for the Israelites as they crossed the desert. Yes, you read that correctly. Water from a rock! "The LORD said to Moses, 'Walk out in front of the people. Take your staff, the one you used when you struck the water of the Nile, and call some of the elders of Israel to join you. I will stand before you on the rock at Mount Sinai. Strike the rock, and water will come gushing out. Then the people will be able to drink.' So Moses struck the rock as he was told, and water gushed out as the elders looked on" (Exodus 17:5–6 NLT).

That. Is. Phenomenal. But that's not all God provided during those forty years that the Israelites roamed the wilderness. Moses sang of God's provision:

> He let them ride over the highlands
>   and feast on the crops of the fields.
> He nourished them with honey from the rock
>   and olive oil from the stony ground.
> He fed them yogurt from the herd
>   and milk from the flock,
>   together with the fat of lambs.
> He gave them choice rams from Bashan, and goats,
>   together with the choicest wheat.
> You drank the finest wine,
>   made from the juice of grapes.
>   (Deuteronomy 32:13–14 NLT)

Sweet, decadent honey from rocks, rich, thick olive oil from the ground, choice meats, the finest wine. This is who our God is and how abundantly He provides something out of nothing for His people!

God provided five smooth stones in a streambed when David was going up against the warrior giant Goliath with only a sling (1 Samuel 17:40). David might have preferred a backup army or a bow and quiver of arrows, but God gave him exactly what he needed to take down the giant.

God provided a loaf of fresh baked bread by Elijah's side when he was exhausted and depressed and fleeing an evil king (1 Kings 19:6). Now, Elijah didn't want bread. He asked God to end his life. Sometimes what we want and what we need are very different. I'm so grateful for a God who knows the difference. After Elijah's nap and snack, God whispered to the prophet in a still, small voice. Later God showed Elijah a plan for his future. One small thing at a time. God provided exactly what Elijah needed to get by in the moment.

God gives us not always what we want but always what we need when we need it.

He'll do the same for us. God gives us not always what we want but always what we need when we need it. Even in the desert seasons. Even when we feel exhausted or less than or like we're not enough or like we don't have enough. It's in the tougher times when I feel like I need more and new and backups and extras—just in case. When I try to take things into my own hands. When I try to fill my insecurities with something I can grab. But God is with us in the good times. And in the hard times. He gives us everything we actually need (Psalm 23:1). Often those things aren't material things at all.

But our world tells us, *More, more, more!* It's December as I write this, and I've been flooded with ads for cute Christmas pj's, sparkly tops, nail polish in rich shades of garnet, and snuggly sheets and pillows with reindeer and holly. These are all things that make me smile. I get sooo into Christmas. And there would be absolutely nothing wrong with treating myself to something fun if I have the resources. But I want to ask myself first, Do I *need* this? Not to be happy. Not to achieve my purpose. Not to have value. I can absolutely still purchase something fun and Christmassy as a celebration of the season, but I want to check my motivations before I add to cart.

We don't need more things to be good sisters or moms or neighbors or wives or speech therapists or professors. We have Jesus. And He calls us His masterpieces (Ephesians 2:10 NLT), not because of what we have but because of how He made us.

Since God promises to provide everything we need, there is freedom in letting go of our excess.

I'm not suggesting that we go sell all our possessions and live in the wild. The new Tree Farm–scented candle I treated myself to makes our home smell delicious. And I honestly feel that God is delighted that I find joy in this candle, that it provides a peaceful aesthetic for our house. What I *am* suggesting is that since God promises to provide everything we need, there is freedom in letting go of our excess and of the false expectation that we need more.

Instead of thinking we "need" another piece of team gear to cheer on our kids or a new outfit for the interview, we can consider what's already in our closets. We can be intentional about what we purchase and the things we choose to keep.

The things we buy don't just cost us dollars. They also cost us room in our drawers and garages. They cost us time to clean and sort and polish. They cost us more time as we're trying to find the right pan in a cupboard jammed with a multitude of other pots and pans, or the perfect top to wear in a closet overflowing with clothes that haven't fit in years. I'm not saying that new is bad or that buying things is evil, but that if we're trying to make space in our lives to be less hurried, getting rid of some physical stuff is a good way to do so.

Jesus tells us how: "What I'm trying to do here is get you to relax, not be so preoccupied with *getting* so you can respond to God's *giving*. People who don't know God and the way he works fuss over these things, but you know both God and how he works. Steep yourself in God-reality, God-initiative, God-provisions. You'll find all your everyday human concerns will be met. Don't be afraid of missing out. You're my dearest friends! The Father wants to give you the very kingdom itself" (Luke 12:29–32 MSG).

Did you see that? How Jesus literally flipped everything on its head? "[Don't] be so preoccupied with *getting* so you can respond to God's *giving*! . . . Don't be afraid of missing out."

Zing!

"The Father wants to give you the very kingdom itself."

Are we soaking in the abundance right in front of us—all that God gives us? Or are we too rushed, trying to find the right lid to fit *that* water bottle, not the other six sitting in the same drawer, before we rush out the door? Are we wasting time securing somewhere to stash our extra art because we've run out of room?

Cleaning out our closets won't solve all our problems. But every item we add to the donate pile is one less thing weighing us down. Every picture frame we get rid of is one less frame we need to keep updated with recent photos. One less thing to dust. Every fun necklace we decide not to buy is one less chain to untangle. One less way we may be relying on things instead of God.

You don't have to give away everything, or even close to everything. You don't have to stop shopping—I love a cute army jacket or floral dress. And some special occasions actually require specific attire. But when we declutter or decline spending, we tend to be better able to "steep" ourselves "in God-reality, God-initiative, God-provisions," because not only are our closets less cluttered; our minds and souls are too.

So, where to start?

Pick a drawer or closet or category of items (such as earrings or socks), and ask yourself these questions:

> Do I need it?
> When was the last time I used it?
> If I don't need it or haven't used it in a while, why am I holding on to it?

Pitch the obvious junk—single earrings and socks with holes. Put the things you love and use frequently back where you found them. The stuff you rarely if ever use can be donated to a local charity. Old hockey equipment from when your son played eight years ago? The French fry slicer you only used once? I find that when I start, I get on a roll. Why again do I have so many purses? Pillows? Pencils? I also find that I never miss the things I've gotten rid of. Never.

When out shopping or when you get that ad in your feed or mailbox, ask yourself these questions before buying something new:

> Do I need it?
> Do I have room for it?
> What else does it require of me?

A coffee maker might also require filters or special pods. A new phone usually means a new case and charger. How much time does it require to dry-clean, have maintenance done, or learn how to operate?

If we get something, because a lamp next to the couch would make it easier to read or those cute jeans would bring us so much joy, can we get rid of something else? If I treat myself to a new article of clothing, I try to put something in the donate pile. You don't have to do this; it's just a way I monitor myself.

God put us in this world and blessed us with our five senses and so many ways to enjoy the physical things around us.

I still have a long way to go. I still get distracted by all the bright, shiny, and cozy things of this world, but I don't want to. Yes, I want to enjoy the goodness God provides for me—savor the flavors and snuggle into sweaters, inhale deeply the rich, inviting smell of coffee when I walk into a coffee shop and curl up with a new novel I'm excited to read. God put us in this world and blessed us with our five senses and so many ways to enjoy the physical things around us. But I don't want to get my worth from things. And I don't want to find security in amassing more things. I want to cling to the fact that my value and provision comes from Jesus. That He already says I'm enough and I'm loved. Not because of my outfit or car, but because He says so. He's the only thing that truly satisfies.

I definitely don't want to slide down the slippery slope the man I knew slid down. Instead of stashing and stealing, I want to steep myself in what God has right in front of me. I want to fully trust His faithful and perfect provision. You and I have the opportunity to get better at this simply by cleaning house.

Does less cluttered sound better? Do God's reality and provision sound inviting? They do to me. In fact, before I finish this chapter, I'm headed to my closet.

Hang on a second.

Okay, I'm back. I grabbed a pair of gold heels and a pair of orange-and-pink sandals, and I placed them both in my donate pile. And it feels good. Freeing. They're both super cute, but I can't remember the last time I wore either. It's been probably two or more years. Don't worry: I held on to my silver heels, so I still have something snazzy to wear at weddings or events.

Start small or start big. But empty some of the stuff out of your life, or set a limit on what you can buy or when you can shop this season. Then enjoy having fewer things to worry about and more of yourself available to notice the reality of all that God is doing in your life and all the ways He provides.

Slow Down

> What I'm trying to do here is get you to relax, not be so preoccupied with *getting* so you can respond to God's *giving*. (Luke 12:29 MSG)

Throw away or recycle five things. They could be magazines you're done reading, shirts that have stains, flat basketballs. You choose. Write down what they were.

Put five things in a bag to give away—books you're finished reading, clothes that don't fit, coffee mugs you won't miss. Write down what they were.

Were you able to stop at five? Or did you keep going? How did the process make you feel?

Thank God for all He gives you, for His provision—for honey from rocks and oil from the ground. Pray that someone else will benefit from what you gave away and that you'll find freedom by letting go.

CHAPTER 8

What Sloths Can Teach Us

Slower Can Be Better

I was watching a nature documentary on sloths with my teenage son and learned that sloths have poor eyesight and hearing and can only walk half a mile per hour on the ground. And yet, these slowpokes have not only survived but thrived in the forests of South and Central America for thousands of years. Their slow pace is a way to conserve energy, and their slow metabolism helps them heal from injuries that might kill other animals.[1]

It got me wondering what I could learn from these cutie-pie creatures. Yes, pauses and breaks are important for my spiritual, physical, and mental health, but what about not only finding rhythms of rest but also doing some things at an intentionally decelerated pace?

Was there anything that I purposefully did slowly?

Is there anything you choose to do in slow motion?

Have we forgotten how to take our sweet time?

We live in an insta-world. We cook things in Instant Pots, share our stories on Instagram, and have our groceries delivered via Instacart.

81

All this instant gratification seems so helpful. I can order jumper cables or that new novel set in France or vitamin C on Amazon and get them delivered to my doorstep. Tomorrow. For free. I can listen to almost any song I like at any hour of the day or night simply by searching for it on Spotify. I can see exactly where my family members are at any moment, all with the cell phone that fits perfectly in my pocket but is too often found in the palm of my hand.

But even in our world where we can check our grades, news feeds, or the weather in real time, or google anything we're curious about, sometimes it's better if we slow our roll. When we embrace some slower-paced activities, we enjoy benefits like being able to focus on what truly matters, staying physically and mentally healthy, and being more productive.[2] But we're not used to slow. Like someone who can't clap in time with the music, we've lost our beat. We have no rhythm. We keep going and doing. As fast as we can.

Some things in life, some very good things, take time.

And yet, some things in life, some very good things, take time. I've recently started dabbling in sourdough. Mixing, kneading, and baking homemade bread is therapeutic for me. A loaf baking in the oven makes the entire house smell amazing, and sourdough has some health benefits as well. But the thing about sourdough is you have to wait for it. All. Day. Long. You can mix your dough in the morning, but it has to rise for at least eight hours. It's not the kind of thing you do if you're trying to whip up a quick dinner—if you're in a hurry. But the result? Warm, fresh-from-the-oven bread? So worth it!

Sometimes slower, as it turns out, can be a marvelous thing. Because a handcrafted latte is way better than a Keurig cup. And homemade tomato sauce that's been simmering on the stove for hours is tastier and tangier and more robust than the kind that comes in a can. Choosing the scenic route home definitely takes longer. But the views? Spectacular! Hiking up a hill or earning someone's trust? They take time. But have rich rewards.

Healing from emotional wounds. Developing healthy relationships. Becoming more like Jesus. All slow processes—things you can't just "speed up" or "rush through" without missing out on integral parts of the journey.

Still, we're not used to slow. So when a slowing down comes along, we can grow antsy and anxious. If we have to wait in line, we often grab our phones and scroll through meaningless content that crowds and distracts our brains. If our direct deposit doesn't hit the second we thought it would, we often grumble and complain. Or if we have to reload a website because it is soooo slow (say it in a whiny voice), we try over and over, getting more frustrated.

But what if, instead, we savored the slow, opened our eyes to see what God has for us in the gradual, the gentle, the deliberate things of life? What if instead of trying to put everything in our lives on fast-forward, we embraced some unhurried activities to experience the richness God has for us there?

Savor the slow, opening your eyes to see what God has for you in the gradual, the gentle, the deliberate things of life.

We can teach someone small how to read or ride a bike. We can work a piece of clay on a wheel until it becomes a bowl or a vase. We can plant seeds, tend to them, water them, and watch them grow. Or we can try to force things to go faster. Maybe even scurrying past important steps or stages of growth or treatment or development so we finish more quickly. And end up with sourdough bread as hard as a rock, projects that look slapped together, and shallow relationships. No thanks.

I love how often we see Jesus taking His time in Scripture.

He was God, so He could have snapped His fingers and made anything He wanted happen in a split second. But He didn't operate that way. On the night of the Last Supper, Jesus took His time. He knew the next day He was going to save the world, but He didn't rush through that evening. Instead, He chose to spend quality time with His disciples, loving them well with intentionality. "Jesus knew that the Father had put all things under his power, and that he had come from God and was returning to God; so he got up from the meal, took off his outer clothing, and wrapped a towel around his waist. After that, he poured water into a basin and began to wash his disciples' feet, drying them with the towel that was wrapped around him" (John 13:3–5).

Jesus knew God had put everything under His power. And still He took the time to prepare for and wash each of the disciples' feet. One by one. Smelly, dirty man feet that had been out walking all day. I picture Jesus washing between their toes, talking to them as He patted first one foot then the other dry. Why does the Bible give us all these details about the steps Jesus did to do this—his clothes, the towel, the basin? Maybe to show us some things shouldn't be rushed.

After the resurrection, Jesus cooked breakfast for the disciples. He could have waved His arms and had that fish roasted and ready, but instead He cleaned those fish—and I don't mean "rinsed them off." Jesus took the time to build a fire and set the fish on the coals (John 21:9–12). And where did He get the bread He served the disciples? We don't know. But Jesus either bought it somewhere and brought it to that place or made it Himself. Maybe it was sourdough. Just saying. Again, He could have done things faster, but He deliberately went through the task at hand.

What is a slow process you're involved in? Getting your degree? Learning a new skill? Making friends in a new city or church? Building up your stamina?

We don't have to take our cues from a culture that tells us we deserve everything right this instant—instant potatoes and instant skin tighteners and get-rich-and-strong-quick schemes. Instead, we can, like Jesus, make and take time to serve and love those around us and ourselves, not in a hurry but with grace. We can take our speed down a few notches and, like the sloths, move at a pace that sustains and heals us. We can knead the dough and stir the sauce and plant the seeds and savor the experiences, breathing in the richness of this full life Jesus always intended for us to live.

Slow Down

> He has made everything beautiful in its time. (Ecclesiastes 3:11)

Do you do anything intentionally and slowly? If so, what do you enjoy about the slower process? Why do you choose to make time for it?

If not, think of something you can do that is slow. Sit and watch the sunset, make a recipe where something has to simmer or rise, paint a canvas, plant some seeds that will need water and light and time to grow.

How do you feel during a slower activity? It's okay if you feel antsy or eager. We're used to a rushed pace. Ask Jesus to help you enjoy the slow and to grow patience, gentleness, and self-control in you.

CHAPTER 9

Off the Grid

Setting Down Your Phone

As soon as we got out of the car, I smelled smoke. Not scary smoke or dangerous smoke, but the inviting, musky smoke of campfires.

I hadn't gone camping since I was in junior high, but smell is intensely tied to memories, and I was flooded with beautiful images of bonfires where we roasted bread on sticks and sang songs to Jesus. I officially accepted Jesus as my Lord and Savior while a camp counselor strummed her acoustic guitar. Now, as an adult, I'd been invited to speak at a women's retreat in the woods. So here I was. I'd never been to this grown-up camp before. But it felt so beautifully familiar.

There were no phones, electricity, or running water on the property. Totally unplugged and off the grid. After an introduction, announcements, and worship under a giant tent, all thirteen hundred women dispersed for some time to sit somewhere quietly by ourselves with Jesus.

At this camp they'd created small handbooks with questions and journal prompts to guide us through our time of silence. I walked with a dear friend into the woods and sat on a bumpy log while she found her own seat. I read through the questions, closed my eyes, and talked to Jesus. I'm rarely without a pen and paper in hand. It's how I process. But here I didn't even do that. I simply sat in stillness under the canopy of tree branches, golden light and God's great love filtering through.

Sitting there, I felt like I could do this every day. Sit in the woods quietly with Jesus. Tell Him about my recent struggles. Fill myself with Scripture that reminded me He is actually the answer to all my problems. There were zero interruptions, because no one was texting or calling, and I wasn't tempted to reach for my phone to see what was going on "out there" because I didn't have it on me. I had no idea what time it was or how long I'd been sitting there. Did it even matter?

Someone in charge would ring a giant bell you could hear throughout the property when it was time for the next teaching or worship session, so any moment between those times was truly just to be experienced, to be present in. I feel so peaceful writing about it now.

I could have taken a million pictures at camp of the women I met, the feast we were served, the handle on my moka pot that melted in the bonfire (thankfully it's still fully functional, whew!). But without a phone, I didn't snap pics; I burned the images in my mind. I could have checked in on my family, but I trusted they were fine. There was an emergency number for the camp I'd given to my husband, so I had peace of mind. Without my phone, my senses seemed heightened. I was less distracted and more present.

I didn't have a phone at junior high camp either. The only phones we had back then had long spiral cords and were plugged into walls. But without photos, I can still picture Tasha, the sandy-colored horse I was assigned to for the week, her coarse white mane, the little white star on her forehead. I can still taste the jugs of orange "bug juice"—some sort of bad, watered-down Kool-Aid we drank at every meal in the dining hall. I can still smell the hay scattered in the corners of the new barn's wooden floors for the square dance we had midweek. There were no texts, calls, or FaceTimes. The only communication I had with home were the two letters I wrote and the two I received from my mom—one of which she wrote and mailed before I left. And sure, I was homesick at first. But I was able to embrace camp for all it was, establish friendships with my cabinmates, and experience things I'd never done before, like hand dipping candles and shooting a bow and arrow. I remember it all so vividly.

Phones aren't bad. As soon as I left grown-up camp, I routed myself home with my map app and called my husband to see how things had gone over the weekend in my absence. That evening, I responded to the group text sent by our campsite host, connecting the eight of us who'd gathered around a campfire for the weekend, sharing stories and praying for one another. I've also followed all those incredible women on social media, so I can continue to get to know them, see what's going on in their lives, and pray for them.

Phones are interrupting our lives.

But phones—and what we do with them—can be distracting and even destructive. We, as a culture, are a bit obsessed with our phones. They are interrupting our lives.

I don't know a soul, including myself, who isn't guilty of sometimes looking down at their phone (or the watch synced with their phone) mid-conversation or when there's a lull in a conversation. We reach for an instant connection with people who aren't there or we don't even know instead of being willing to mine a meaningful conversation with the people in front of us.

Were there pauses in my conversations around the campfire? Yes.

Did they always fill with someone asking another question or sharing another story?

Yes. Eventually.

And the stories were hilarious and meaningful and bonded us. Our chatter ranged from favorite meals and upcoming trips to health struggles, major job decisions, marriages, infertility, nursing babies, what we were most longing for, and what we desperately wanted Jesus to show us.

Is every conversation in life easy? Of course not. But what if we stuck with them? Asked one more question? Waited one more moment for someone to respond to something we said? What if we took the extra time to communicate better instead of looking for the quick fix of instant interaction? What if when conversations don't come easily, we tried a little harder, were a bit more authentic, instead of reaching for our crutches—ahem, I mean phones?

How much time a day do you spend on your phone? Many phones will send you a little report at the end of each week, which can sometimes be alarming. And sure, I use my phone to Face-Time my kids, map my route, and listen to worship music while I run. All good things that add up to hours of phone usage. But I also check my email too often, spend more time than necessary on social media, and look up too many random facts that have zero bearing on my life.

Some of that time I waste on my phone could be used to slow down, to find more intentional time with Jesus.

Most of us have busy lives. We're struggling to find time to do things we want to do, like prayer or reading the Bible. Yet most of us waste some time each day on our phones. There are literally people whose jobs are to keep us online to click the next article, view one more post, and stay on our feeds a few minutes longer, because then we'll see another ad or two. Even when we plan on simply finding out what other movies that actress has been in, we find ourselves saying, "Oh, she was in that? Who did she play? Who else was in that film? Oh gosh, that's her husband? I didn't know she was married to that guy. Do they have kids?" And we lose another five or ten precious minutes.

There are literally people whose jobs are to keep us online to click the next article, view one more post, and stay on our feeds a few minutes longer, because then we'll see another ad or two.

"Smartphones are useful tools," states Loren Brichter, inventor of the pull-to-refresh mechanism on so many sites. "But they're addictive. Pull-to-refresh is addictive. Twitter [now called X] is addictive. These are not good things." He goes on to say, "I regret the downsides."[1]

Zoinks! That's the guy who invented the feature that when you're looking at your feed and hoping someone new has commented or messaged or scored a goal, you pull down on your screen. He regrets the thing he invented. He admits it's addictive.

I don't want to be addicted to my phone. Or anything except for Jesus.

"Two billion people will have thoughts that they didn't intend to have because a designer at Google said, 'This is how notifications work on that screen that you wake up to in the morning,'" says Tristan Harris, former design ethicist at Google.[2]

Jaron Lanier, a computer scientist, says, "It's the gradual, slight, imperceptible change in your own behavior and perception that is [social media companies'] product."[3]

I know, I know. Those are some scary quotes. The tech insiders in Silicon Valley admit they're manipulating our thought patterns. But wait, Christians! We're not supposed to be conformed to this world or our phones or some random techies in California. We're supposed to be turning to Jesus for guidance and inspiration, because He's greater than anything in this world (1 John 4:4).

The apostle Paul reminds us, "Do not conform to the pattern of this world, but be transformed by the renewing of your mind. Then you will be able to test and approve what God's will is—his good, pleasing and perfect will" (Romans 12:2).

The Message version of this same passage in Romans puts it this way: "Don't become so well-adjusted to your culture that you fit into it without even thinking. Instead, fix your attention on God. You'll be changed from the inside out. Readily recognize what he wants from you, and quickly respond to it. Unlike the culture around you, always dragging you down to its level of immaturity, God brings the best out of you, develops well-formed maturity in you."

I don't want to be dragged down by culture or manipulated by Silicon Valley. Do you?

Adults spend two to five hours a day on their phones. (For teens, it's five to eight hours.) We crave the hit of dopamine we get with another like or text or notification. We find satisfaction in those hits and self-worth in those pings, and we doubt our self-worth when our phones sit silent. If we pick it up, open an app, check our email, pull down, play another round, will it show us that somebody likes us, is interested, noticed?

Ick! I don't want to feel that way.

We can choose to let Jesus be the one who renews our minds.

We don't have to. We have the power of the Holy Spirit living in us. We can choose. We can choose *not* to be conformed to the patterns of this world. We can choose to let Jesus be the one who renews our minds. We can put down our phones and turn off our notifications. We can delete apps and turn off ringers. We can declutter our social media feeds by unfollowing people we don't know or who aren't healthy for us to follow. We can put old-fashioned alarm clocks in our rooms and wake up to them instead of grabbing our phones first thing.

The Bible warns us about distractions. Peter got distracted by the waves of the sea while walking toward Jesus, and he started to sink (Matthew 14:30). Paul warned the early church to stay focused on Jesus and *not* get distracted by the earthly things around them: "Since, then, you have been raised with Christ, set your hearts on things above, where Christ is, seated at the right hand of God. Set your minds on things above, not on earthly things" (Colossians 3:1–2).

We can set our minds on things above or on earthly things. Where are we looking?

Paul instructed another church, "Be very careful, then, how you live—not as unwise but as wise, making the most of every opportunity, because the days are evil. Therefore do not be foolish, but understand what the Lord's will is" (Ephesians 5:15–17).

Are we being foolish or wise? Are we making the most of every opportunity or getting sucked into the black hole that lives inside our phones?

To clarify, I'm not saying phones are the root of all evil. They're not.

Satan is.

I have a phone. I use my phone. I'm on it every day. I use it for a lot of good things. But my phone is also a distraction. And its addictive qualities keep me on it, make me check it more than I'd like. Picking up my phone interrupts my work, my prayer time, and my time with people around me.

As we're trying to slow down to find more time to quiet our minds, more time to spend with the Lord, reducing our phone usage is a quick and easy way to start. I'm not insisting we all go to the woods for a camping weekend and leave our phones behind, although it was blissful. But I'm guessing all of us could reduce our phone time by fifteen minutes a day and not miss a single thing.

And with that extra fifteen minutes, we'd be a little less rushed, a little less distracted, a little less influenced by people we don't know, a little less stressed. We'd have a little more margin. We'd listen a bit better, feel more rested, notice our surroundings more fully, discover something new. Which to me sounds peaceful, like some quiet time alone in the woods or sitting around a campfire and praying with friends.

Slow Down

> Don't become so well-adjusted to your culture that
> you fit into it without even thinking. Instead, fix your

94

attention on God. You'll be changed from the inside out. Readily recognize what he wants from you, and quickly respond to it. Unlike the culture around you, always dragging you down to its level of immaturity, God brings the best out of you, develops well-formed maturity in you. (Romans 12:2 msg)

Go to your settings on your phone and check your daily usage.

Map out a plan for reducing your screen time by fifteen minutes a day this week. You could set limits on apps that distract you, snooze your phone from a certain time each evening to a certain time each morning, choose a day each week to go phone free, or dedicate certain times of day that are off-limits (such as meals or when you're with others). Some of these will work for you and others will not. Find what does work and start eliminating some of your distractions.

Choose how you'll use your freed-up fifteen minutes, not with another task but with prayer, stillness, a catnap, Bible reading, time outside, or some other sort of rest.

CHAPTER 10

It Is Finished

Time to Move On

"It is finished." These were Jesus's last words on the cross (John 19:30).

And it was. His assignment on earth to be the living sacrifice to erase the sins of humanity was finished. Jesus gave up His life for us. And all those who believe this beautiful truth were redeemed in that moment.

Jesus loved His disciples (13:34), but His time with them was coming to an end. Jesus loved His mom (19:26–27), but His time of being her earthly son was complete. Was there still work to do to spread the good news of God's kingdom? Were there still people to be healed, saved, and taught? Absolutely!

But it was time for Jesus to return to heaven to do all kinds of amazing work that He still does today, like offering us peace, grace, hope, and love. In order to do that, He had to complete His earthly ministry.

Jesus's days of walking around in His sandals, sitting by the campfire with the disciples, and preaching to crowds were over. And He knew it. Not because Jesus didn't like that work or those days but because God had something new and different for Him.

So Jesus said, "It is finished," and moved on to the next things God had laid out.

Jesus said, "It is finished," and moved on to the next things God had laid out.

Jesus did this.

But do we? Do we keep doing the things we're doing, working the jobs we have, living where we live, just because we've been doing it like that for a while? Even when it's time to move on to something else?

I was on the board of a performing arts organization and positively loved it. I took ballet growing up, am a huge music fan, and adore theater (*Hamilton*, anyone?). I'm basically enamored with the performing arts. The board was made up of interesting and intelligent members of our community. We met once a month, ate delicious snacks, discussed upcoming performances, and helped plan an extravagant black-tie fundraiser.

But the meetings always seemed to be scheduled at inopportune times for my family. We were juggling several rides and car pools for our kids in order for me to attend. I also didn't feel like I was contributing. I soaked in the exposure to the arts, listened to fascinating stories from other board members, ate decadent brownies, set up tables and a red carpet for our fundraiser, but didn't know if I was making a difference. It seemed like others in the community could contribute more. I kept getting this feeling from God that even though I enjoyed the board, I could use my time and gifts in better ways to live out the calling God had on my life. So I stepped down. And said goodbye to the brownies and discounted show tickets. *Sigh.* It was finished.

Then you know what happened? Instead of feeling the stress build up each month prior to a board meeting, I lived in the freedom of not worrying if I could attend or how we were going to juggle two other activities to make it work. I also found I had more time to be present with my husband and kids and had more space in my mind to write.

In the Bible, God asked people all the time to lay down things for something else He knew was better. God asked Joseph, who lived in Israel, to leave the life he knew in his home country and up and move his wife and baby to Egypt, to protect them from being killed (Matthew 2:13).

Now granted, God asking me to lay down my responsibilities on that performing arts board was nothing in comparison to God telling Joseph to move to keep Jesus alive. But similarly to how God told Joseph, "Living in Israel was great, but now I need you to move, because it's not good for you anymore," God let me know, "There was a season to be on the board, and now it's not the best use of your time anymore. Step away, into something better." This simple shift freed my mind and some chunks on my calendar. I don't regret my time on the board. It was just time for it to be over.

What is it time for you to move on from? What might God be asking you to step away from?

Right as Joseph was getting acclimated to Egypt, God asked Joseph to move his family again. And again.

> After Herod died, an angel of the Lord appeared in a dream to Joseph in Egypt and said, "Get up, take the child and his mother and go to the land of Israel, for those who were trying to take the child's life are dead."

So he got up, took the child and his mother
and went to the land of Israel. But when he heard
that Archelaus was reigning in Judea in place of his
father Herod, he was afraid to go there. Having
been warned in a dream, he withdrew to the district
of Galilee, and he went and lived in a town called
Nazareth. So was fulfilled what was said through
the prophets, that he would be called a Nazarene
(Matthew 2:19–23).

God told Joseph to move two more times!

Personally, I'm not a big fan of moving. Of sorting through and
packing all our belongings, of searching for a new home and a
new church and a new dentist. But if God asks us to say goodbye
to something, there is a reason—a really good one. God had a
purpose in asking Joseph to move all three times. The relocations
kept Jesus safe from evil tyrants *and* fulfilled the prophecies of
the Messiah. As always, God knew what was best.

*If God asks us to say goodbye
to something, there is a
reason—a really good one.*

He knows what's best for you too.

Have you been volunteering somewhere for ages even though
new causes tug more at your heart? Planning the cookout for the
neighborhood you moved away from four years ago? Hosting
Christmas for your extended family even though your niece has a
new home and has hinted she'd love to host a family get-together?

Eating that food even though it always gives you a stomachache? Living in a home that doesn't fit your current life stage?

Maybe you *should* keep up the work or the tradition, keep sharing yourself in this way. Maybe Jesus is calling you to stay right where you are. But maybe, just maybe, it's time to pack up your bags and free up some space in your life so you can follow Jesus to the next adventure.

Like physical things, responsibilities pile up. We're in a club, and then we get asked to lead the club. We help with a conference, and the next year we're asked to plan the conference. Soon we find ourselves annually leading and planning. Things can spiral. These might even be good opportunities, but they're not what we originally agreed to, and too many commitments can crowd up our calendars, potentially blocking our view of Jesus's vision for us. If we're too busy in our current roles, it's tricky to take a moment to evaluate how we're spending our time.

Like physical things, responsibilities pile up.

Sometimes we worry things won't continue—or won't continue *well*—if we walk away from them. Who will know that client's name or that his daughter rides horses? Who will be able to make Nana's sweet potato recipe like she did? Can anyone else really teach the class you designed? But if Jesus calls us onward, shouldn't we be confident that Jesus has everything under control?

When Jesus asks us to make a change, things will be different, but why do we worry that they might be worse? Jesus will still love, encourage, strengthen, and provide for us whether that's in a new neighborhood, office space, or stage of life.

Are your current responsibilities keeping you from what Jesus is calling you to do next?

Have you been doing the thing God once called you to do, but maybe you got stuck in a rut? Or is your work finished in Israel because it's time to move on to Egypt? Or Nazareth? Are your current responsibilities keeping you from what Jesus is calling you to do next? Is it time to release something?

I can't answer that for you. But Jesus can. Joseph didn't walk away from his home without God's prompting. I didn't quit the performing arts board—or my job in corporate real estate, or the book club I was once in—without Jesus nudging me: *Is this the best use of your time?*

Ask Jesus. He has a perfect plan for you no matter what stage of life you're in. He's gifted you with specific talents and resources for specific purposes. And sometimes it's time to use those gifts that have served well in one area somewhere else. If you seek His advice, He'll let you know. Because Jesus always wants what's best.

If you feel like Jesus is calling you forward, maybe it's time to move, start something new, pass the baton, create an initiative, or form a new team. Or maybe it's time to step back, rest, take care of your mental or physical health, or focus on a relationship. Maybe it's time to say, "It is finished," freeing up space in your life to follow Jesus to a new adventure.

Slow Down

It is finished. (John 19:30)

Make a list of all your current responsibilities—your job, volunteering, family, church commitments, and so on.

Pray over your list and ask Jesus if there's anything He'd like you to walk away from. The answer might be no. This idea of stepping away from certain responsibilities might not be for right now but for the future.

If the answer is yes, ask Jesus to help you figure out how to lay down that thing.

Thank Jesus for giving you good work to do. Let Him know that you want to do it as long as it pleases Him and no longer. Ask Him if He has something new for you that you should be clearing space for in your schedule.

PART 2

Refuel

The number one class ever taught at Yale University was Psychology and the Good Life. Over twelve hundred students at a time have been enrolled (one-fourth of the entire undergraduate campus!). The course became so popular Dr. Laurie Santos, who created and taught the class, turned it into a free online curriculum for workplaces, teens, everyone. Because we all want to live a good life. Don't we?

Dr. Santos said, "Our intuitions about what will make us happy, like winning the lottery and getting a good grade—are totally wrong."[1] So in her class, Dr. Santos teaches topics like savoring our lives, getting outside, practicing gratitude, engaging in meditation or prayer—things that psychologists have found actually lead to a happier life.[2]

Interestingly enough, God knew way ahead of science that these things are good for us, that they help us live an abundant, joyful life. They're all biblical. They're all ways of connecting with Jesus.

Everything we talked about taking out of our lives in the first part of this book are things that inhibit us from living our best lives. In this section we'll discuss some things we can add into our lives (now that we've made more room on our calendars and in our brains and in our souls) that will help us discover true joy.

None of the ideas in this part are meant to be items we check off a list or feel guilty about if we aren't incorporating them into our days. But they're all biblical practices of spending time with God, remembering and grounding ourselves in how very much He loves us and wants goodness for us. They all grow the fruit of the Spirit—love, joy, peace, patience, kindness, goodness, gentleness, forgiveness, and self-control—in our lives. These ideas give us renewed energy and fill our tanks. They refuel us to do the good work God calls us to do, engage with the people we care about, and fully embrace this one wonderful life God's given us.

Personally, I want all of that!

Now that our tanks are a little less clogged with excess, let's refuel with the good stuff, the high-octane love and grace of Christ, and head into the good life.

CHAPTER 11

Quiet Time

Silence and Solitude

I had four babies in less than eight years. There was a snapshot in time when I had an eight-year-old, a five-year-old, a two-year-old, and an infant who I was nursing. All while my husband was in grad school getting his PhD. Let's just say I was tired. No. *Exhausted.*

There was no need for an alarm clock because my five-year-old was a self-starter and woke up around 5:30 a.m. all by himself each morning. And so the day began. It was filled with cuddles and giggles and picture books that my kids and I adored. There were crafts and trips to playgrounds and snacks—so many snacks. In the summer we'd go to the pool almost daily. Which was refreshing and a welcome change of scenery from our family room but also exhausting. Watching one child go off the diving board while another wants you to watch them do a handstand underwater while another really needs a super vigilant eye despite their floaties while you're trying to keep your baby's head above water, interspersed with running all of them to the restroom at different times, can wear a mama out.

I loved every single splash, snow cone, smooch, and sandbox adventure. But every day I looked forward to quiet time.

It was originally nap time when my oldest was our only child, and that was easy to navigate. "Now it's time for your nap," I'd announce. Then I'd give her a kiss, swoop her upstairs, change her diaper, read her favorite board book—*Snoozers* by Sandra Boynton—and lay Maddie and her special soft blankie with the tiny pastel puppy-dog pattern in her crib. "Mommy loves you. Night night."

By the time our youngest was born and Maddie was eight, she was too old for naps. But I still needed a break. Now more than ever. So, I established quiet time. For a precious hour and a half every afternoon, I laid down the baby and toddler for their naps, and the rest of us went to our rooms and were quiet. Could you read to yourself? Sure. Could you play make-believe school with your stuffed animals or baby dolls? Of course. Could you *click click* your Lego bricks? Absolutely. As long as everything was turned off and everyone was quiet.

As soon as the kids were situated, I'd exhale. Because I needed that quiet. It was solace for me. Sometimes I'd nap. Sometimes I'd read. Sometimes I'd get something done that was uber-challenging with littles, like cleaning toilets, making phone calls, or dicing vegetables.

This time without noise refueled me, so when everyone emerged from their rooms, I'd be energized and excited about smearing thick, gooey blobs of bright blue, yellow, and red finger paint on white paper or baking brownies or searching for acorns in the yard.

What ever happened to quiet time?

Silence is something we don't get a lot of in our culture, but scientists have proven that when we turn down the noise, it can help our body, mind, and spirit. Potential benefits of silence include improved concentration and focus, lower blood pressure, brain cell growth, the calming of racing thoughts, increased creativity, reduced cortisol (the stress hormone), and better sleep.[1] Which all sounds a-ma-zing.

But our culture is really noisy. Even when life feels quiet for a moment, we often turn on a television for "background noise," or play some tunes in the car, or listen to a podcast to pass the time. Which are all fine.

Our souls need to be quiet sometimes.

But . . . it turns out our souls need to be quiet sometimes. That in the quiet we reduce stress and boost our brains. Yes, please. Quiet time was critical to my sanity as a young mama, but we can take it a step further than simply turning down the noise. We can intentionally seek Jesus in our silence. When we do, it can help us feel His presence, understand our value and purpose, and hear His voice and instructions for our lives more clearly.

Throughout the Bible we find people hearing God's voice in the quiet. For example, Moses was tending sheep (Exodus 3:1) and Gideon was threshing wheat (Judges 6:11–16)—doing their work, hard work—when God gave them incredibly important directions to lead His people. Those men could hear God so well in the silence. But it's interesting—neither of them was seeking quiet. Silent opportunities were just a way of life.

There are also examples where Jesus's followers intentionally removed themselves from the noise of everyday life to hear God.

When the apostle Paul first met Jesus, he started preaching in Damascus. When some of the Jews there plotted to kill him, Paul took off by himself to Arabia (Galatians 1:15–17). Paul went away for safety, yes, but also Paul spent that time alone with the Lord, listening to the voice of Jesus. And he came back invigorated.

Paul went on to undertake four arduous missionary journeys and plant at least fourteen churches. There's no record of what happened while he was alone with God in Arabia, but Paul came back strengthened, empowered, encouraged, and emboldened to do the good work God called him to do.

In the book of Acts, Peter also found a quiet, alone place to be with God in the midst of the work the disciples were doing to spread the good news of Jesus. "About noon the following day as they were on their journey and approaching the city, Peter went up on the roof to pray. He became hungry and wanted something to eat, and while the meal was being prepared, he fell into a trance. He saw heaven opened and something like a large sheet being let down to earth by its four corners. It contained all kinds of four-footed animals, as well as reptiles and birds. Then a voice told him, 'Get up, Peter. Kill and eat'" (Acts 10:9–13).

It was here alone on a roof that Peter heard God speak to him out loud. God soon revealed to Peter that the words He spoke meant Gentiles were welcome in the kingdom of God. At the time this was revolutionary. Peter was able to hear something from the Lord that was completely countercultural in the silence of a rooftop.

Sometimes silence and solitude are like this. We sense God giving us an important message, maybe giving us an instruction or an idea. Sometimes we're reminded that God is with us and that His power lives in us, empowering us to do great things when we work with and for Him.

And other times silence and solitude simply help us pause. Or dump some of the things we've been holding on to. Or begin processing thoughts we didn't even know were issues. Or catch our breath. These peaceful moments to allow our soul to catch up with our body are just as important to our well-being and relationship with God as the revolutionary ones.

In the quiet we are positioning ourselves to be in tune with God's voice and feel His amazing grace.

God won't force us to turn down the volume, but He has goodness waiting for us in the quiet.

We need to be intentional if we desire quiet. We have access to sound 24-7. Our shows, movies, and music stream anytime, day or night, and presto, we have entertainment, opinions, and knowledge at our fingertips and in our ears. God won't force us to turn down the volume, but He has goodness waiting for us in the quiet. And we can choose. We can choose to turn off our devices every now and then. Really. It's a thing. Our phones have off buttons.

We also have phone calls that need returned and that interview we're supposed to watch before class. We have family members who need advice or a meal. But it's not selfish to take a pause from our responsibilities and relationships to find a moment of silence. Obviously, sometimes chatting with a loved one or attending that meeting is the very best use of an afternoon. But prioritizing some quiet with God?

It's priceless.

It helps us love our families and friends better, because it helps us remember how loved *we* are by God. It helps us do our work better, because we're reminded that our work has meaning and purpose. It helps us get through the hard things, because our minds are momentarily rested and we're more centered in Christ's peace. God invites us into moments of quiet because He knows it restores us, and He wants that for you and me.

We can find a quiet place and listen to Jesus.

Where is that quiet place for you? How can you make that happen? You'll need to figure out what works for you, and it might take some trial and error.

Some days I go out on our porch and sit in one of the Adirondack chairs in silence, trying to still my swirling thoughts. Other days I drive in silence instead of making a call or playing music. I might pray for whoever I'm driving toward, for our conversations, for me to shine Christ's light where I'm going. Or just let my mind and soul take a break. The same holds true when I go on a run. Often I'll jam to worship tunes or listen to an audiobook I've been wanting to hear. But sometimes when life feels loud, when I've gone from one thing to the next, when there's a lot on my mind, I'll choose to run with nothing but quiet in my ears. On hectic days my quiet time might even be when I pull into the garage, park the car, and close my eyes for a minute, breathing deeply, before I get out and dive into whatever awaits me inside.

Jesus quiets worries and puts things in perspective.

It is in this quiet that an unwinding happens. A disentangling of the three zillion thoughts I have each day—the paperwork for my daughter's scholarship, the yucky conversation I had with a family member that keeps replaying in my head, the fact that I need to swing by the store because we're out of garbage bags, the wedding I need to RSVP to, the thing I'm praying fervently for a friend. The silence is where the thoughts run their course and file themselves into manageable folders in my mind with the help of Jesus.

In the quiet God speaks to me about what's important, and I can hear Him better because I've pulled some of the noise that was drowning His voice out of my proverbial backpack. Jesus quiets my worries and puts things in perspective. He listens to my ideas, hopes, concerns, and dreams, and getting them out of my system is settling. The silence is where, after two or twenty-two minutes, I sometimes hear God tell me, "I love you." Or, "Move on." Or perhaps, "Don't make that call today." He might say, "It won't be worth it without Me." Or, "I'll give you what you need." Or simply, "Trust me." God might remind me, "I created that person." Or, "I'm proud of you." Or I might hear one way or another about a decision I'm making. Things I never would have heard if I'd chosen noise over quiet.

Sometimes I sense these things. Sometimes I don't. Sometimes I simply hear silence. But knowing Jesus is listening while I sift through all those thoughts in my brain always helps. It's a start. I feel better than before I entered into silence.

When my kiddos were little, sometimes the baby cried during quiet time, which evolved into three pairs of small eyes peeking out from their doors. There were days when one or all of us were sick and needed extra care. Or an event fell smack in the middle of quiet time. On those days we missed it. It happens.

It happens in our silence with God too. Don't beat yourself up if you miss a day, or if most days you find quiet at lunch but on Thursdays your office has mandatory lunch meetings. Maybe in your current situation quiet is near impossible to come by, but on Mondays you sit in your car by yourself while the kids you carpool run their drills. Then take full advantage of Mondays.

God has always known what science is figuring out: silence is good for our bodies and souls.

God isn't angry if you can't make it every day or if you change it up. God's not taking attendance. He just loves it when we show up. God has always known what science is figuring out: silence is good for our bodies and souls. And silence with Him is priceless.

On the days I missed quiet time with my kiddos, we all felt it. They were a little grumpier and didn't play quite as nicely with each other. I was tired and had less patience. The same holds true when I miss silence now. I'm a little more on edge, a bit more antsy, and not as confident in who I was created to be. I lose sight of the fact that God is in control and His plans are perfect. I'm more easily frazzled or thrown off. I feel the difference in my spirit.

Silence in this noisy world isn't easy to find. But when we seek it, it is so very worth it, like a breath of fresh air, or a hug from someone we love, or the first flower we see bloom in spring after a long, cold winter. It stirs hope within us, joy. After a dose of silence, I'm more in step. I'm less worried and more content. More calm. More gentle in my soul. More of who Jesus always intended me to be.

Slow Down

Be still, and know that I am God. (Psalm 46:10)

Do you often get quiet? If so, where and when?

If not, brainstorm with God how you might be able to do that. Can you find quiet in your shower? Can you park far away and find silence as you walk to your building? Can you linger in the lobby and sit in silence for five minutes before entering or exiting the office?

Try setting a timer for five minutes and sitting with zero noise. Did the time go quickly or slowly? What did your brain do? How did it make you feel?

CHAPTER 12

A Gorgeous Photo of Paris

Prayer

Here is a sample of three miscellaneous texts my husband sent me last week:

OTG in CVG

I think I misunderstood. I'll call you after mtg

[*Photo of the rose window at Notre-Dame cathedral*]

The first was to let me know he was on the ground in the Cincinnati airport, whose airport code is CVG, to keep me posted and ease my mind until we could speak.

The second was an honest acknowledgment that texting isn't the ideal way to communicate, and therefore he wasn't sure what I meant by the five words I texted him earlier. To avoid misinterpretation, he would call me after his meeting.

The last is one of the ways Brett tells me he loves me. I love Paris, and just the sight of it makes me sigh. So sometimes Brett sends me a random gorgeous photo of Paris to interject loveliness into my day.

Texting isn't the key to staying in love, but whenever anyone asks Brett and me our secrets to a happy marriage, we always give the same response:

1. Have Jesus at the center of your marriage. He has to be on the throne for it to work.
2. Communicate all the time about everything.

Texting is a great and convenient way to communicate, although as illustrated by example number two, it's not the best way. A call is better than a text. FaceTime is better than a call. And face-to-face conversation, phones down, distractions put away, is the very best. But on days when one of us is traveling or in meetings, texts are a wonderful way for Brett and me to stay connected. A text is way better than no interaction. It says, "I'm thinking of you. I want to share something with you. I care about what's going on with you. I love you."

If I didn't talk to my husband for a week, that would be difficult. I know because there have been instances when he's traveled to developing countries for his research, and due to time zones and almost-nonexistent cell service, we've had to go days without talking. It was rough. When we did connect during those trips, there was so much to share but limited time, so we couldn't get to everything. We weren't able to express all the important emotions we'd experienced or share all the silly little things that had taken place.

It usually took a few days of Brett being home for us to unravel all the thoughts and get back in sync with one another. I was never sure where to start. Should I ask about the people Brett met? How he was feeling? What he learned? Should I begin with the big picture things he needed to know? What part Maguire got in the play? Mallory being selected team captain? How one of our kids really struggled with him being gone? Should I share the disappointment I faced? How about that cruel thing someone said to me? Should I keep it to myself and not bombard Brett with my stuff? For goodness' sake, he just got back from Sri Lanka.

Brett's brain would also be full of thoughts he wanted to share and questions he wanted to ask and news he hoped to know. Neither of us knowing where to start was clunky. And then, like two junior high kids at a dance, one of us would say one thing, like a step to the left, and the other would blurt out something random, which leaned us a bit off-balance. Then we'd both say something different at the same time, stepping on each other's feet, and we'd laugh, and even though we were offbeat, we'd start to dance again.

The same principle holds true for our relationship with God.

God isn't judging our conversation skills. He just wants us to communicate with Him.

It is a relationship after all, and therefore communication is key to keeping it healthy and flourishing. If we go for long periods without talking to God, it might feel a bit stilted or like we don't know where to start. But it's all right. God isn't judging our conversation or dancing skills. He just wants us to communicate with Him.

Jesus talked to God the Father all the time. Jesus prayed before feeding thousands of people with one boy's lunch (John 6:11). Jesus prayed in the morning (Mark 1:35). Jesus prayed in the evening before making the very big decision of choosing His apostles (Luke 6:12–13). Jesus prayed during His last meal with His disciples (John 17). Jesus even prayed on the cross (Luke 23:34).

God wants to hear all of it. You can start with the small thing that's bugging you or making you giggle. You can blurt out the thing you're worried or scared about without any lead-up. You can begin by thanking God for being available, for wanting to be with you, or even by saying, "Hi God, it's been a while, but I want to talk."

God's ready and listening with open, loving arms at all times.

God's ready and listening with open, loving arms at all times. Yes, God knows everything because He's omniscient. But even though I *know* my husband loves me, I love to hear Brett say it out loud. And even though I *know* Brett knows I adore Paris, every time he sends me a picture of Paris, it makes me smile. And even though I *know* one of my kids is grumpy because their math test was hard, I like it when they tell me, when they let it all out and rant about the problem that was "impossible to solve" and that "no one finished the test." Because I know it helps them to talk about it. Because then I can better understand the nuances of why it upset them. Because I can better parent and love them when they tell me.

God's the same way. He just wants us to talk to Him.

If you have no idea how to begin, the Lord's Prayer—or the

Our Father, as some traditions call it—is a great place to start. It's the framework Jesus gave His followers on how to pray. Jesus never meant for it to be the only way we pray, but it is a classic. Jesus said:

> This, then, is how you should pray:
>
> "Our Father in heaven,
> hallowed be your name,
> your kingdom come,
> your will be done,
>   on earth as it is in heaven.
> Give us today our daily bread.
> And forgive us our debts,
>   as we also have forgiven our debtors.
> And lead us not into temptation,
>   but deliver us from the evil one."
> (Matthew 6:9–13)

Jesus gave us this prayer as a template. It pretty much covers it: giving God glory, remembering who God is and the authority we want Him to have over our lives, asking forgiveness for the ways we mess up, reminding ourselves to let go of the grudges we hold, asking for God's protection and provision. Amen!

This is an awesome prayer. A prayer for before you start your day, meeting, game, or commute. A prayer for your scheduled quiet time. But like it helps me to communicate with my husband throughout the day, not only when he gets home from work or a trip, the same holds true for our exchanges with God.

When an email pops up in my inbox and I know it holds important information by the sender's name or subject line, I want to take a moment to ask God to step in. I might say, *God, whatever this email holds, please help me cling to you. Thank you for loving me and for knowing in advance how this should play out. I pray your will, not mine, be done. Amen.*

When I'm headed to the hospital for the follow-up mammogram, I pray for God's peace to flood me, for a clean bill of health. I pray in advance that if things are not clear, that the radiologist will find whatever needs to be found, for quick and successful healing, so I can tell people the story of how Jesus healed me. I also pray for anyone suffering with breast cancer to know God's great love for them, and for the scientists working on a cure that they can make wonderful discoveries to heal bodies and change lives.

I could go on and on about the times I need and want to pray. As the apostle Paul summed it up, "Pray without ceasing" (1 Thessalonians 5:17 ESV).

We might schedule talking to Jesus as part of our normal routine—before dinner or bed or when we wake up. We might have long, heartfelt conversations with Jesus because something came up. A one-on-one sit-down is, of course, the very best way to talk with your heavenly Father. But He also loves it when you FaceTime, call, or text—well, actually their equivalents. Prayer can be a quick thank-you, praise, or plea for help as we make it somewhere safely, hug a friend, get lost, or are confronted and don't know what to do.

Words can't always express how we're feeling.

But words can't always express how we're feeling. Sometimes in our hearts there is a sensation of goodness or beauty or longing or fear or desperation, and we send those ideas and emotions to the God who gave them to us. Praying is just like communicating with people we love, so it's different at different times depending on the situation and what we want to say. I have friends who write out Scripture as prayers and others who sing worship songs as prayer. The important thing is *that* we pray—not how or when we pray.

We're all works in progress at this prayer thing. If the way you're praying doesn't seem to be working, that's okay. Why not try to figure out what's wrong? If my phone screen is locked, I don't throw away my phone. I bet you don't either. We figure it out. We turn it off and on. We ask a friend for help. We google the problem on another device. If we're that diligent about making our little pocket computers work, shouldn't we put the same effort into making our prayer lives work?

If sitting down to pray indoors makes you zone out or fall asleep or get jittery, that's okay sometimes. I've definitely fallen asleep while praying, which is fine. It meant my body really needed rest and I got some. But if it happens all the time? Try changing it up. Pray outside or while you walk or bike by yourself. If you feel stuck in your routine of praying in your head, maybe start praying out loud. Try keeping a prayer journal and write out your prayers and anything you sense from God on the pages. You could even highlight or circle answered prayers to remind yourself of the ways God listened, was active, and tended to your needs.

Will your mind wander during prayer? Of course. I hope it does. Because when you spend time with a friend, doesn't your conversation jump from topic to topic? They share a story that reminds you of something else, and then that prompts them to tell you who they ran into. The same holds true with your conversations with God. You might start by praying for healing for a family member. But then you start thinking about everything you need to get done today, so you ask God to show you how to prioritize your time and for some peace in the process. One of those things on your to-do list is to cook something for your small group, and God reminds you that a group member has a gluten allergy and you'll need to plan accordingly. With that thought solidified, you move on to another friend who asked for prayer.

It's part of prayer. Letting those random thoughts out, sifting through them, finding answers, letting go of some things, asking God questions one by one and allowing Him to direct you.

If you're super distracted every time you pray, get creative. You could pray in the shower or while you mow the grass. I have a friend who prays for her family members as she folds their clothes. Another friend prays for her clients before working on projects for them.

Talking to God is one of the most important things we can do each day.

You might find that all or none of these approaches work for you in your current season. Keep experimenting until you find one that does. Talking to God is one of the most important things we can do each day. When my youngest was still at home while the bigger kids were at school, we'd spend hours playing Legos. When my little boy's brain got immersed in his play, I'd sit next to him and use that time to pray.

Change it up throughout the day, week, month, year. See what resonates. Maybe some types of prayer work better when you're tired or excited or sad or on weekdays or on weekends. Great! Keep pursuing the ones that work. I have a friend who in a traumatic season of life stopped by an old cathedral each morning on the way to work, slid in a pew, and poured out their heart to God. That beautiful place felt holy. They were better able to connect with God there. Another friend who experienced serious church hurt found that reading the Psalms out loud was the only way she could pray for a season. So she read them on repeat, and by doing so she kept communicating with God.

There are no prayers too big or too small for God to handle.

There are no prayers too big or too small for God to handle. We can pray for healing of a headache or a tumor. We can pray for ourselves, someone we care about, the acquaintance we bump into, or a complete stranger. Jesus healed the blind, lame, and deaf. He healed people with skin diseases, physical and mental ailments, shrunken hands, cut-off ears, and demons. Jesus even raised people from the dead. He is mighty and loving and can take on any prayer we've got.

We can pray for more energy when we're run down. We can praise God for a hot fudge sundae or ask for guidance for a decision or wisdom for world leaders or peaceful ends to wars. We can pray for our kids' teachers or for blessings on a conversation with a friend. Jesus cares about every detail of our lives. Even the hairs on our heads are numbered (Matthew 10:30), so nothing is too minute to talk to God about. He can do more than we can ever hope or imagine (Ephesians 3:20). Why not ask Him for it?

Let's bring Jesus our dreams and fears and worries. Let's tell Him about the little thing that made us laugh and the other thing that got on our nerves (although we know we should let it go). Let's spend some time going deep with Jesus, like a long conversation over coffee with our best friend, and also let's give Jesus a quick thanks in our minds for how delicious that coffee is. At some point in our day, let's tell our faithful God we love and appreciate Him. Not unlike the way my husband sends me a gorgeous photo of a red-canopied café dotted with cane-backed chairs, the Eiffel Tower visible in the background, to remind me that he loves me.

Slow Down

> Pray without ceasing. (1 Thessalonians 5:17 ESV)

Do you have a prayer routine? If so, what is it? If not, how might you add prayer to your day?

What types and styles of prayer have worked for you in the past?

Today, intentionally set aside ten full minutes for prayer. Maybe try a new way of prayer or one you haven't tried in a while.

Try sending text-like prayers to Jesus at least three times today. Just a quick "Thanks" or "Help" or "Wow" or "Peace, please."

Note how you feel before, during, and after your prayer times. What worked? What didn't? Did you hear or feel anything specific from God?

CHAPTER 13

Their Names Are Tricky

Reading the Bible

As my online counseling appointment was coming to a close, I scribbled notes furiously. My therapist had given me some lists of things that trigger people with PTSD (that's me). I was supposed to circle anything on the list that triggered me and then rate how extreme my reactions were. Simple enough.

Except that as I read down the list, I circled more and more items. Arguments? Check. I avoid them like the plague. Please don't ever get mad at me. Wanting all the blinds open? Check. I thought that was just because I like sunlight. You get the idea. I've been seeing my counselor for years, so it isn't that I'm completely unaware of what some things from my past have done to my psyche. But when I started with my therapist, she helped me stop the bleeding—the things that needed immediate attention for my emotional health. And that was good and I'm grateful. But now we're deconstructing the damage those wounds did. And although important, it's not super fun.

My therapist and I set up our next appointment and disconnected our call. I sat in a pile of papers I'd printed with purple writing scrawled all over them and a profound understanding of how much work I still needed to do to care for my mental health, how much I still needed to heal. I thought I'd made good progress. I *had* made progress. And yet I felt shaky.

Our appointment had been first thing in the morning, and I hadn't had time to finish my morning Bible reading before it began. So I set aside the worksheets and opened to my bookmark in 2 Kings 19, a passage about evil King Sennacherib of Assyria who threatened King Hezekiah of Judah. Both kings' names are tricky to pronounce and kind of made me want to skim over the text. But I didn't, knowing that if I stuck with it, I'd find God in these pages. I always do.

The living Word of God never returns void (Isaiah 55:11). When we read the Bible, God can always show us something, teach us something, enlighten us, encourage us, equip us for something later. God promises that if we show up, He'll use our time in the Bible for good. So, I read. Even the tongue-twister names. And at the end of an exhausting chapter of accusations, threats, and sieges, I read this: "That night the angel of the Lord went out and put to death a hundred and eighty-five thousand in the Assyrian camp" (2 Kings 19:35).

One short sentence reminded me that my God has the strength, cunning, and capability to take down an enemy army of 185,000 soldiers in one fell swoop. I was comforted by His power, that this power is on my side.

A few verses later in 2 Kings 20:7, the Lord answered Hezekiah's prayer and saved the king who had become deathly ill. And in verse 11, God moved a shadow on a sundial. All these facts seem unrelated:

a battle victory
a healing
the king getting some time back, which means God actually
moved the sun to manipulate time—wild!

But they're all miracles. All reminders of God's powerful, capable, mighty self to a girl who was feeling overwhelmed by how her past can sometimes make her anxious and on edge in her day-to-day. God used these chapters in 2 Kings, which are rarely discussed or quoted. I don't think I've ever heard a sermon on these three miracles. But that morning I felt God saying to me, "Hey, look, I've got you. I'm a conqueror. I'm a healer. I'm a miracle worker. Time is on *my* side. I control it. This past trauma doesn't have to be too much to process, because you're not processing it on your own. I'm here with you. And I can do anything."

It's not always like this. I don't find comfort for all of my specific concerns every time I open Scripture. But the Bible is alive and active (Hebrews 4:12). And God always uses it for something. Reading my Bible is the time each day when I recalibrate to what truly matters, to who I am, to who God is and what good news that is. It's refreshing and refueling and helps me navigate my day.

Jesus used Scripture to explain who He was, to help crowds better understand answers to their questions, and to resist temptation.

Don't take my word for how centering and nourishing Bible reading is. Jesus Himself knew Scripture inside and out. Jesus referenced Noah and the flood (Genesis 6–8), Jonah getting swallowed by a big fish (Jonah 1), King David (1 and 2 Samuel), and the queen of Sheba (1 Kings 10; 2 Chronicles 9), and He frequently quoted the prophets and Psalms. Jesus used Scripture to explain who He was, to help crowds better understand answers to their questions, and to resist temptation. If Jesus valued Scripture so much, and we're trying to follow Him, shouldn't we check it out?

When we read the Bible and talk to God about what we read, we can fill up on truth and anchor ourselves, so we aren't swayed by the lies of culture or frenemies—or even the lies we tell ourselves. The more we read the Bible, the more we understand the free life Jesus offers: a life where we don't have to perform, a life where we don't have to say yes to everything, a life where our value has nothing to do with how full our schedules or bank accounts or closets are, a life where we can savor His abundant gifts.

Here are some examples of what I mean.

Pop culture and social media give us definitions of what we should look like and how we should present ourselves. And there's social pressure to attain that look. But the Bible says we were made in the image of God (Genesis 1:27). When we read this and meditate on this, we become free from comparing ourselves to others. We're made in God's image! We don't need to be taller or shorter or have straighter hair or stronger arms. We don't *need* that color in our spring wardrobe or that brand of shoes to be wonderful. We don't need to be louder or quieter or funnier or more serious. We already are wonderful because God specifically created us how He intended us to be. What a beautiful truth. How freeing is that?

When we read our Bibles, we also learn that God promises to never leave or forsake us (Hebrews 13:5). Never. Because so much of our social interaction is online instead of face-to-face, we can sometimes feel lonely. But this truth defeats the lie that we are alone. Because Jesus is with us. Here. Now. When we spend time in His Word, Jesus reminds us of this.

And on the days when we're fighting battles—because we will have physical and mental health battles, work battles, and relationship battles we're fighting—the Bible reminds us we're not fighting alone. God equips us to fight well and victoriously. Ephesians 6 tells us we can stand strong in the Lord and in His mighty power (v. 10) and that God's full armor is at our disposal (v. 11). We aren't empty-handed. We don't need to rely on our own strength. We can stand in God's strength and fight wearing His armor.

On the days when we're fighting battles, the Bible reminds us we're not fighting alone.

Psalm 65:5 tells us God is the hope of everyone on earth. I'm on this earth. Are you? Then this includes us. We aren't hopeless, even if some days we feel like our situations are, because God promises to provide us with hope.

I need these truths in my arsenal. I need to pull these verses out of my pocket on dark days, long days, exhausting days, wonky days, and days when I get thrown a curveball. The more we read the Bible, the more we familiarize ourselves with these truths. The more they sink in. The more readily they come to mind when we need them.

Do you read the Bible every day? Or do you wonder how in the world you could fit in Bible reading when the twins are hyperactive, or the event you're in charge of is less than a month away, or you've gotten texts from eight different people all asking for some of your time this week?

If you're currently struggling to find time to read the Bible, give yourself some grace. God's not mad at you. He just knows there's more peace and joy and love waiting for you if you read your Bible. Also, don't try to go from zero to reading for an hour a day. Start where you are and grow from there. As with any good habit you hope to form, it helps to set aside a specific time each day to make it part of your routine. Is there a time when you can slow down? Is that first thing in the morning? Great! Right before you go to bed? Awesome! At your desk at two in the afternoon when you're starting to feel restless or sleepy? Perfect. You get to choose. You know your schedule. When works best for you to open your Bible?

Try to find time when you can be alone, or at least alone in your head. If you commute on public transportation or call the local coffee shop your office, the mass of humanity may be buzzing around you, but it could also be a perfect place without interruptions where you can read and contemplate God's Word. To me, reading the words on a page is more powerful than any other format, but I have friends who listen to the Bible while they get dressed or during their drive time. God's living Word being read over them feeds their souls.

If you ask Him, God will help you find a time and a way to read the Bible.

Finding time by yourself may be easier said than done, but you can do this! God is with you. Are you a full-time caregiver and feel like you're never alone? You can still pull out a children's Bible and read it to your kiddos during snack time or read out loud to your elderly loved one after lunch. If you ask Him, God will help you find a time and a way to read the Bible.

How much time should you set aside? If you're starting out, maybe search for five minutes. Everyone has five minutes. It's simply a matter of prioritizing. That could be while the roast is in the oven, while you're sitting in the waiting room, or while your roommate, spouse, or child is using the shower you share.

How much should you read? Again, it's up to you. Sometimes I read only a couple of verses, contemplating them, journaling about how these promises impact my life. Sometimes I read an entire book of the Bible (like one of Paul's letters) in one sitting to let its overarching message sink in. You'll need to figure out what works for you. It's about connecting with God, not about how many pages or chapters we achieve.

The Bible is called the living Word of God for a reason. It is alive. God uses it to speak directly to you and me. There are days when I'm reading and, wow, it's as if the author who wrote the passage thousands of years ago knew exactly what I needed in this moment. Like that morning after my counseling appointment when I needed reassurance. Or sometimes what I read is super applicable for what a friend is going through—like in the "Art of Saying No" chapter when my husband read about manna and shared that Scripture with me. God knows what we need to hear and makes those words jump off the pages when we need them.

I admit there are days when I read about genealogies and boundary lines of nations and wonder how all that applies to me. Other times I'm physically exhausted, so even though I'm reading, it's difficult for the words to sink into my sleepy brain. But it's the consistency of this exchange—me reading God's Word, God speaking through it—that builds my relationship with Him, that makes me more in tune with who He is, His character, and the love, joy, and peace He offers.

It's like how I communicate daily with my daughter who lives in Nashville. Sometimes we have deep, meaningful discussions when I visit her or she comes home. Other days we exchange the highlights over the phone, touching base, shooting a quick text, always saying, "I love you." This consistency builds and strengthens our relationship. This is the kind of foundation that's built through daily Bible reading. This ongoing dialogue with Jesus strengthens us in times of trouble, helps keep us from stumbling, and pulls us up when we fall.

Inserting the daily rhythm of reading our Bibles isn't just one more thing to cram into our already busy schedules. It's the opposite—a breath of fresh air, something that refreshes and grounds us. A daily dose of God's Word helps anchor us to the truth that Jesus loves us and inspires us to act accordingly. Taking time to fill our minds and hearts with truth that defines, soothes, strengthens, and restores us is a game changer. We read to remember. We slow down to read the words to remind ourselves of who God is and who He says we are.

Slow Down

> My word . . . goes out from my mouth:
> It will not return to me empty.
> (Isaiah 55:11)

How often do you read your Bible?

If you don't read the Bible regularly, pick a time and place where you can spend five to ten minutes in the living Word of God each day.

Not sure where to start? The gospel of John is a great starting point since it's a biography of Jesus. I also love Philippians and Ephesians for seeing why Jesus makes a difference and how we, as Christians, are called to live.

If you already read your Bible, recommit to making this time even more fruitful. Perhaps you could increase the time, add journaling or prayer, read a new translation, or read a commentary along with the Bible to help further explain the text.

CHAPTER 14

Friday Mornings

Worship

Our son Max lived at home his sophomore year of college. We literally live one mile from campus, so it was easy enough. Max is a musician, specifically a worship leader, and was involved in a ministry on campus called Friday Morning Worship. It was exactly what it sounds like. On Friday mornings college kids gathered to sing worship songs, praise Jesus, and pray. At 7:00 a.m. I mentioned this was college kids, right?

The student who had hosted Friday Morning Worship the previous year graduated, leaving this ministry homeless. Max asked if we could give it a new home—our home. Brett and I agreed. On Thursday night I did a speedy wipe down of the bathroom and vacuum of the family room. My husband pushed the coffee table against the wall to create more space, and Max set up his keyboard and speakers. On Friday morning the coffee pot was gurgling next to the handful of mismatched mugs I'd set out, sending the inviting smell of java throughout the house.

And by 7:10 a.m. our family room was packed.

Students in hats and hoodies filled our home. Although we're close to campus, you can't walk to our house along the narrow fifty-five-mph country road leading from the university, so they all had to find rides. Yet here they were. I counted over fifty pairs of Vans, flip-flops, Crocs, and Converse scattered by our front door. Each and every owner of those shoes was in our family room singing and whispering and shouting phrases like "All glory to Him!" and "Thank you, Jesus!"

Week after week throughout the school year, this was Friday morning at our house. The beautiful sound of voices lifted to God. Different students with musical gifts taking turns leading the group. In the winter, students wrapped themselves in the fleece blankets we had sitting out. Some students darted out early each week to make it to 9:00 a.m. classes. Others lingered, sometimes until afternoon. Some days we had doughnuts.

And whenever possible, I joined in. Some Fridays I'd sit and pray while the music washed over me. On others I'd dance around the kitchen, joy overflowing from my heart. Most often, I'd stand and sway and sing, tears streaming down my face as I took time to focus on Jesus. On who He is. On what He's done. On what that means. For me. For the people I love. For you.

As you've probably gathered by now, I love Jesus. I am beyond grateful for what He's done, how He's rescued me, how He changed my entire life trajectory and continues to flood me with love and grace I don't deserve. And yet no matter how big a part of my life my faith is, there is something powerful about *singing* to Jesus that undoes me. And I can't carry a tune.

It's not that I don't know the truths I'm singing. There's nothing surprising for me in the lyrics. But it is the intentionality, the pause, the stopping of everything else simply to sit at my King's feet and adore Him. When we sing words saying that we're here to worship Jesus, that He is our Lord, that He is great, that He is holy, we aren't just taking in the information; we're declaring it. We're using not only our minds but also our bodies to encounter

Jesus. We're immersing ourselves in these truths. Claiming them out loud. Solidifying them in our hearts.

***

> ## When we sing words declaring that we're here to worship Jesus as our Lord, that He is great and holy, we're immersing ourselves in these truths.

The Psalms repeatedly invite us to use our mouths to sing praise to God:

> My mouth will speak in praise of the LORD.
>   Let every creature praise his holy name
>   for ever and ever.
>   (145:21)

> Open my lips, Lord,
>   and my mouth will declare your praise.
>   (51:15)

> He put a new song in my mouth,
>   a hymn of praise to our God.
>   (40:3)

> Sing to the LORD a new song;
>   sing to the LORD, all the earth.
>   (96:1)

And God's people throughout the ages have modeled this for us. Deborah and Barak sang a song of victory over their enemies

(Judges 5). Hannah sang a song of thanksgiving after God answered her prayer for a child (1 Samuel 2:1–10). Paul and Silas sang to God even while in prison. While they were singing, the prison walls shook and crumbled, the doors flew open, and everyone's chains fell off (Acts 16:25–26)!

At the Last Supper, Jesus held the cup and bread, and told the disciples to take and eat and drink. Then, "when they had sung a hymn, they went out to the Mount of Olives" (Matthew 26:30).

Jesus sang worship songs.

Of course! Jesus knew singing to the Lord was good. And Jesus modeled this kind of worship, this singing worship, for us.

Science is catching up. Several studies show that singing together directly impacts endorphins and other neurochemicals in the brain, reducing pain, increasing productivity, improving mood, reducing stress, and making people feel more connected.[1]

Music is powerful. Music focused on Jesus is even more powerful.

Have you felt this? You're visiting relatives and attend church with them. The service feels so much different than what you're used to. Then the musicians go into a worship song you know, and your shoulders relax. Instead of feeling out of place, you feel more comfortable because you found God in the music, and when you're with Him, you're always at home. Or you hear an old, familiar hymn you haven't heard in ages and start singing along. You didn't even realize you knew the words, but they hold special territory in your brain. Or you walk into the sanctuary frazzled, running late, just having dropped off your kids in kids' ministry—and they did *not* want to go. But as you slide into a seat, you notice yourself humming or singing along to the worship already in progress. The music finds a way through your stress and distraction and points you back to God and how much He loves you.

Music is powerful.

Music focused on Jesus is even more powerful.

And when we take part in it, we step away from stress and self-consciousness and toward grace and light and belonging.

My husband and I visited his mom, who suffers from Alzheimer's, yesterday. When we arrived, she asked, "Do you know me?" Later in our time together I started singing "Jesus Loves Me," and she joined in singing every single word. Her muddled brain struggles to remember her family, but she can still connect to Jesus through song, because the effect of music is crazy significant. This blows me away.

God put music within our hearts and souls as a way to commune with Him.

There are so many wonderful ways to connect with Jesus. Worship is just one of them. And for the record, worship isn't confined to singing. We'll talk about other kinds of worship in the next chapter. But worship in the form of music is powerful. Many theologians believe the very first song was God singing creation into existence.[2] God put music within our hearts and souls as a way to commune with Him. Are we tapping into this amazing gift?

Worship music can be old-fashioned hymns on a pipe organ or modern hymns or worship tunes played on an electric guitar. You can "sing to the LORD a new song" by attending a worship event, going to Sunday service, playing piano and singing as your fingers move across the keys, or singing along to worship songs while you cook dinner, mow the grass, or make your morning commute. You don't need to have Friday Morning Worship in your house, although you could start it. What's stopping you?

Friday Morning Worship is one of the most beautiful and authentic things I've experienced. (If you want to hear what a family room full of college kids worshipping sounds like, find "You Saved Me" on the playlist at the back of the book.) This year Max lives in a house off campus with seven other students. They host Friday Morning Worship at their house. But I still drop by whenever possible. Before my Friday gets busy. Before my weekend begins. I put myself at the feet of Jesus and thank Him for all He is. I remind myself of His love and grace. I sing these truths out loud so my heart and soul remember.

And I usually have mascara running down my face when I leave.

Slow Down

> When they had sung a hymn, they went out to the Mount of Olives. (Matthew 26:30)

Do you sing to the Lord?

Find at least one way to make a joyful noise to the Lord this week. That can be playing a worship song or hymn on an instrument, writing a song of your own, singing along to the radio, asking

Alexa to "play worship music," finding a YouTube video of a worship service and kneeling or singing or praying or dancing along, or maybe even hosting or attending a worship event with others and declaring the goodness of God.

CHAPTER 15

Without Singing a Note

Other Forms of Worship

I promised you we'd talk about other forms of worship besides singing—nonmusic worship. So here we are. What can we do to worship God without singing? Well, according to Romans 12:1—everything. "So here's what I want you to do, God helping you: Take your everyday, ordinary life—your sleeping, eating, going-to-work, and walking-around life—and place it before God as an offering" (MSG). We're supposed to take our everyday lives—our sleeping, eating, going to work, and walking around—and use them for God's glory as a "living sacrifice" (v. 1). The apostle Paul tells us this is "true and proper worship."

Today I understood how this plays out.

I made my high school boy cheesy eggs for breakfast, added a piece of homemade pumpkin bread with chocolate chips I'd baked earlier this week, then placed some blackberries on his plate along with his vitamins. This is not his normal breakfast. I rarely get all fancy like this at 6:00 a.m. But this morning I had an extra minute, and it brought me joy arranging it all, knowing it would make him happy—a treat on a dark, chilly school morning. I was feeling incredibly grateful to Jesus for this kid, and it made my heart so full that I could do a little something to start off my boy's day a bit brighter.

When Maguire left for school, I made myself a mocha and read my Bible. This morning I was in Esther and read the famous challenge from Mordecai to his cousin, Queen Esther: "Perhaps you were made for a time such as this?" (see 4:14). This verse always hits me hard, and today was no exception. I felt empowered. *Perhaps I was made for a time like right now. Jesus, what do you have in store? I'm ready. Let's go!* This time in my Bible was worship. I was so aware of how God empowers us and gives us purpose, and I was so grateful to Him for it.

Later I went on a walk with my friend Shena. Bundled in hats and mittens, we paused our movement and our conversation as a baby deer and its mama crossed in front of us. We took in the grace and beauty of these creatures, amazed at how very close they were to us. Once the deer made their way back into the woods, Shena and I laughed and exchanged stories and some genuine struggles too. We pointed out the golden leaves and gushed about how much we love where we live and how beautiful it is in autumn, praising God for His creation. When we got back to our cars, we prayed for each other—right there in the parking lot. I started by thanking God for this friendship, for this time together, for how I always see parts of Jesus when I'm with Shena. This was all worship—the walking and talking and laughing and sharing and, yes, the praying too.

I wrote some of this book this afternoon, so grateful I get to be a writer. It's what I always wanted to be when I grew up. *Thank you, Jesus, for making me a bookworm and growing my love of books and stories into this.*

You get the gist. It was all worship.

Yesterday? Not so much.

Yesterday I woke up with a migraine. My husband's car wouldn't start, so I needed to take him to work. Which I was glad to do.

His office is only one mile from our house. But it somehow made my morning feel a bit off, not how I thought it would look. And because of the headache, it all felt like an inconvenience, even though it was not at all. Other than that, I had a similar day: I made breakfast for my son (a much simpler one), brewed a coffee, went for a run in the woods, put the finishing touches on a blog. But each task felt like something I needed to get through instead of a blessing I got to be a part of. It felt like a rock was pressing against my left eye socket and I might throw up at any moment. I couldn't even think clearly.

I found a prayer for when you're sick in a book of liturgies and prayed the words someone else wrote, asking God for pain relief and thanking Him that a headache was the worst of my woes. I prayed for friends and strangers who suffer from chronic pain, aware for a moment of how much they must struggle on the daily. I prayed that God would somehow use me even in this.

I tried. But my everyday, ordinary life didn't feel very worshipful. It felt like just getting through. And that's okay. Because Jesus saw me in my migraine. He saw me trying to pray. And today Jesus gave me a clean slate, with a clear head and a joyful heart able to worship Him anew.

Listen, we're not going to get this right every day.

But we can keep trying. Not striving. But showing up.

We work worship into our muscle memory.

Because when we show up, we get better. We work worship into our muscle memory. Using our life to worship Jesus becomes our very best habit. So even with that migraine, although I didn't feel overly grateful, I felt a teeny bit of gratitude. Even though I didn't intentionally make each thing I did a way to serve God, I turned to Him. Even when I couldn't find words to pray in my own mind, I found the words to pray in a book. It was important to me, because I've learned when I make room for prayer in my life, it changes things. For the better. Because I've practiced worshipping, I eked out a bit of worship without even realizing it, even on a crummy day. It's becoming part of my normal rhythms.

Not all the time. I still fail at this frequently. But the more I intentionally slow down, sorting through what doesn't matter to make room for what leads me into a life worth living, the more I find myself seeking worship almost instinctively. So on the bad days, we can assess where we are and try to reset accordingly. And then, hopefully, in a day or two we'll get back on track to more intentional worship, because it's our usual habit.

No matter what's on your docket today, you'll have opportunities to worship God.

No matter what's on your docket today, you'll have opportunities to worship God.

Changing diapers, changing tires, and changing lanes can all be acts of worship. Taking out the trash, taking up a collection, and taking someone's temperature can also be worship. Finding time for a friend, finding a cure, and watching *Finding Nemo* can all be acts of worship.

How do we do this? By making them things we do for Jesus, for His kingdom. By being grateful for the people and tasks God has put in front of us. It's all about our mindset.

Whether you have a trip of a lifetime planned for today or you're staying home on the couch recovering, you can worship Jesus. We can slow down in the moment to thank God for the ways He provides for and protects us. We can ask Him to help us steward our situations well. With prayers like this, we'll be in the right mindset to take our everyday, walking-around life to worship Him. We can dedicate each act to God and His glory.

We can dedicate each act to God and His glory.

I don't know what your today looks like. I'm working this morning and then headed out of state for my daughter's afternoon soccer game. I'll heat up leftovers for a late dinner for my family on my return. I can take this day and praise God for it—for all the opportunities and situations that come my way. I can worship Him. And some of the time I'll remember. And some of the time I'll get frustrated or tired or want things to go my way. But the more I practice Romans 12:1, the more I'll be able to reset and take this "everyday, ordinary life . . . and place it before God as an offering" (MSG).

So can you. We can start by simply praying: "Dear Jesus, thank you for this day, for the sun rising, for breath in this body. Please help me use this day for your glory. Please help me be aware of and grateful for all you give me. Please keep my mind and heart open and aware of how to further your kingdom in any way, big or small. I love you and acknowledge every good thing I have comes from you. Amen."

Slow Down

> So here's what I want you to do, God helping you: Take your everyday, ordinary life—your sleeping, eating, going-to-work, and walking-around life—and place it before God as an offering. (Romans 12:1 MSG)

What's on your agenda today?

Ask Jesus how you can pause and use whatever tasks you need to complete today and whatever interactions you'll have with others, planned or spontaneous, to worship Him, to thank Him for this life and all that He enables you to do.

CHAPTER 16

How Long Should You Look at a Sunset?

Receive Goodness

"Have you seen the sunset?" my husband asked as he walked in the door with our youngest son.

"No, should I?" I asked, but I was already wiping my hands on the kitchen towel and headed outside. He wouldn't have asked that question unless there was something spectacular going on in the sky.

The sun was almost finished with its nightly performance. It sat low, almost touching the horizon. Dark violet, deep tangerine, vivid crimson, all trimmed with gold, illuminated a strip of sky. Beautiful. I exhaled and turned to go back inside. But I felt a tug to stay one more moment, and as I pivoted back toward the magnificent artwork God created that evening, I heard Jesus speak to my soul: *Receive.*

Receive. As in, *Fully receive this beauty.* Don't take a glance and keep on going about your day, your life. This. Is. Spectacular. Here is a glimpse of glory. Hold on to it. Why would you consider walking away?

But we do, don't we?

Here is a glimpse of glory. Hold on to it.

We're so busy going to the next thing and the next that we don't always take time. In fact, we get in seasons when we rarely pause to receive any of the goodness God puts in front of us.

Our heavenly Father has created so much beauty, so much goodness: the melody of rain falling, the smell of cinnamon rolls baking, the warmth of sunshine on our face, music that makes our feet tap, conversations that nurture us. Are we receiving these gifts? Do we make time to receive them? Do we even remember how?

The world-famous artist Georgia O'Keeffe, known for her paintings of flowers, commented, "Nobody sees a flower—really it is so small—we haven't time—and to see takes time, like to have a friend takes time."[1]

Wait! I don't want to miss the flowers or sunsets or a friendship or any of the other glorious things God has given me because I don't think I have time for them. If we're too busy scrolling through our feeds, trying to get to the next level or step, checking things off our lists, we might miss these spectacular gifts God intended for us. And wouldn't that be tragic?

"Rejoice in the Lord always. I will say it again: Rejoice!" the apostle Paul instructed the church in Philippi and us (Philippians 4:4). Paul went on to tell them how to do this: "Whatever is true, whatever is noble, whatever is right, whatever is pure, whatever is lovely, whatever is admirable—if anything is excellent or praiseworthy—think about such things" (v. 8).

You might be thinking, *Easy for you to say, Paul.* Maybe you're in a situation that doesn't exactly make you feel like rejoicing. Maybe you're struggling to see anything lovely or pure in your life. Paul totally gets that. He experienced shipwreck, rejection, and poverty. And as he wrote this letter, instructing the church to rejoice always, he sat in jail. I'm guessing in the first century, that wasn't exactly glamorous. It was dark and damp, and there were most certainly rats. Paul was awaiting trial with the possibility of execution looming over his head. And yet, Paul speaks of a true, inner joy. He says he's been able to find contentment in every situation—his high highs and low lows (vv. 11–12).

We can do all things through Christ's strength—even find complete joy in a jail cell.

Paul explains that the secret is Jesus. That we can do all things through Christ's strength—even find complete joy in a jail cell. Because there is always something true or noble or right or pure or lovely or admirable to focus on no matter the circumstances. Because Jesus is good and loving and full of light and truth.

Something lovely could be a sunset, like the one my husband suggested I look at. Glancing at it is one thing, but gazing at it is another thing altogether. Allowing the beauty to fill me. Marveling at it.

Something true could be meditating on Christ's promise that no matter what is going on in your life, you are fully and totally loved by Him.

Something pure could be a pristine white snowfall outside your window. Gaze at it. Consider it. God still creates bright, beautiful things in this world—unspoiled, breathtaking.

We can find hope in these lovely, true, pure things. We don't need health, wealth, or everything figured out to focus on loveliness. It's all around us. If only we'll slow down to notice.

The thing I've found is that the more I look for things that are true, noble, right, pure, lovely, admirable, excellent, or praiseworthy, the more I find them. And the more I'm aware of all this goodness, the more filled with joy I become. I notice the woman leaning over the tiny blue bicycle with her young son riding as she pushes it along. I see love in her dark eyes and devotion in her actions and delight in her son's face as he zooms along the path. I spy foxtail grass growing along the edge of a field and reach out, allowing my fingers to be tickled against the fuzzy caterpillar-shaped ends. I hear the laughter bubbling up in my daughter's throat before it fully escapes, and I can't help but smile as I feel her contagious joy.

The more I look for things that are true, noble, right, pure, lovely, admirable, excellent, or praiseworthy, the more I find them.

God puts beauty and goodness all around us to restore us. Jesus knows that when we focus on noble and pure and excellent things, our hope is renewed. We become thankful for what we have. We become encouraged by the wonderful things and people all around us, even when there is hardship or darkness in our lives. This shift of our attention from the pain or tension to beauty reminds us that God is still there, and He's still doing good things.

Some days I don't think I deserve all this goodness. It feels selfish to indulge in a half hour on the couch to read a chapter of a really good book with a steaming cup of peppermint tea, letting the mug warm my hands, because shouldn't I be getting dinner started, folding laundry, vacuuming the stairs? Or it might feel irresponsible to enjoy the luxury of a long, hot shower, allowing the peony-scented bodywash to relax me. But it's usually not.

Yes, we all have responsibilities. I'm not trying to dismiss them. My family needs to eat, preferably in clean clothes. But what good is a clean house if no one sits down to enjoy living in it? And of course you need to do the work God puts in front of you. But I doubt a long shower will make or break whether you get those papers graded or that stack of résumés reviewed. In fact, a steaming shower might be exactly what you need to clear your headspace to complete your work well.

You see the disconnect?

If we're constantly rushing, we'll miss joy. But if we pause and focus on what is true, noble, right, pure, lovely, admirable, excellent, or praiseworthy—if we receive it, savor it, inhale it, let it soak in—we'll be filled with abundant, overflowing joy that will fuel us to do the things that really matter.

I choose the latter. To work from a place of joy. To truly see and smell a flower.

Care to join me? I'll be out on the porch gazing at the sunset.

Slow Down

> Finally, brothers and sisters, whatever is true, whatever is noble, whatever is right, whatever is pure, whatever is lovely, whatever is admirable—if anything is excellent or praiseworthy—think about such things. (Philippians 4:8)

Look around right now for something that is true, noble, right, pure, lovely, or admirable. If there's not something visible that's lovely, close your eyes. Is there something delicious you smell? Something soft to touch? Something you know to be true from the Bible, like the fact that Jesus is the light of the world (John 1:9) or that His love for you endures forever (Psalm 136:1)?

Now spend three minutes thinking about that thing—about how pure the coo of a mourning dove sounds or how the leaves seem to actually dance as the wind wafts through them.

Thank God for His goodness that is truly all around. Ask Him to use the goodness you've experienced to fuel you.

CHAPTER 17

Shake Mistakes

Biblical Fasting

When I was in high school, my mom bought SlimFast. I'm not sure if the name SlimFast meant that it was supposed to help you get slim fast or that it involved fasting to get slim. Either way, when my mom started the SlimFast diet, I joined her. In the cafeteria, I drank the shake I'd packed, which sort of tasted like chocolate milk, and then was hungry and grumpy, craving the fries on my friends' lunch trays.

It was my first experience with intentionally not eating, and it was awful. The plan permitted you to eat one meal a day, and you drank SlimFast shakes as substitutes for your two other meals. I was a teenager who pored through fashion magazines, gazing at airbrushed models, and was unhealthily obsessed with body image. I also did ballet and was on the school dance team and was burning way too many calories to limit my intake. My body should *not* have been "dieting."

Thankfully my SlimFast-ing only lasted two days. Whew.

Fasting to get closer to Jesus is a whole other thing. A way better thing. For way better reasons. Biblical fasting has nothing to do with numbers on a scale or a pair of jeans and everything to do with understanding how much we need Jesus, how much He provides for us.

Biblical fasting has nothing to do with numbers on a scale.

People are fasting left and right throughout the Bible. Moses fasted when he received the Ten Commandments (Exodus 34:28). Esther fasted before approaching the king (which meant risking her life), in an attempt to reverse the genocide ordered on her people (Esther 4:15–16). Even Jesus fasted before His temptation in the wilderness (Luke 4:1).

Jesus said to a crowd listening to Him "when *you fast*," not "if *you fast*."

Jesus flat out assumed the folks He spoke to fasted, because He said to a crowd listening to Him "*when* you fast," not "*if* you fast." "*When you fast*, do not look somber as the hypocrites do, for they disfigure their faces to show others they are fasting. Truly I tell you, they have received their reward in full. But *when you fast*, put oil on your head and wash your face, so that it will not be obvious to others that you are fasting, but only to your Father, who is unseen; and your Father, who sees what is done in secret, will reward you" (Matthew 6:16–18, emphasis added).

"When you fast" . . . as if everyone in this crowd could use some advice on the subject because it was part of their regular routine.

People in the Bible fasted to get ready for some really big things. They also fasted hand in hand with prayer. It was a regular thing for them. And fasting has continued to be a beautiful way to walk with Jesus. Renowned Christians like Martin Luther, John Calvin, C. S. Lewis, and Dietrich Bonhoeffer all practiced fasting.[1]

Fasting isn't something we talk about much as Christians today. When I was growing up, our church never even mentioned it. Besides my bad SlimFast shake incident, I had never tried it. But a few years ago, God did a thing in me. The concept of spiritual fasting kept popping up. It started with that Bible passage we just looked at where Jesus says, "When you fast." Then fasting was a topic in a book I was reading. And then I listened to a sermon that "happened" to discuss fasting. Not long afterward, a friend described her experience of fasting to me in a random conversation.

It felt like God *really* wanted me to know about fasting, so I did more research. Turns out Christians for centuries have been fasting to "draw near to God, deepen one's relationship with Him, and seek His help in times of special need."[2] I want to do all those things. Draw near to God. Deepen my relationship with Him. And seek His help.

But also . . . fasting isn't for everyone. As my pastor often says, "The Bible was written *for* you, but it wasn't written *to* you." When Jesus said, "When you fast," we have to consider who He was saying that to. Jesus was talking to a culture that wore long robes that covered their entire bodies every day. Women's ankles were even covered. Nobody knew what size anyone else wore. Clothing sizes weren't even a thing back then; they just popped on a loose robe that kind of flowed around them. There were no airbrushed pictures of pop stars or models or influencers. There was no social media. No filters on photos. No swimsuits. No shorts.

No one would have known I have a varicose vein running down my left thigh from when I was pregnant with Max. No one would ever have seen the scar on my knee from a bad roller-skating incident when I was a kid or have a clue that I'm short waisted. No one would have known anything about your body either. Jesus was talking to a culture that was not obsessed with their bodies.

But our culture? In our culture, 75 percent of all women will experience disordered eating behaviors in their lifetime.[3] In our culture, twenty million American women will suffer from an eating disorder. In our culture, we know what way too many people's bodies look like, and we obsess over comparing ours to theirs.

Fasting is simply one way to get closer to Jesus.

Fasting was never meant to be a way to jump-start a diet, have control over something when things feel out of control, or alter our bodies in any way. Fasting is simply one way (out of so very many) to get closer to Jesus. If you are pregnant, or struggle with disordered eating, or are diabetic, or have any other medical issue where not eating for a day or so could throw things out of whack, fasting is most likely *not* for you. Abstaining from something else could be a great alternative to fasting in order to grow the fruit of the Spirit of self-control and increase your gratitude (two things fasting is wonderful for). You could abstain from social media or shopping or eating out, and instead use those moments when you're abstaining from those things to get closer to Jesus.

All that in mind, if you think fasting is something you'd like to try, it can be beautiful. But be intentional. Choose a purpose for your fast. You can use it like the people in the Bible to prepare for something big, like a move. Or to help you make a decision. Or to focus on a specific prayer request, like your friend who's going through chemo, or women suffering injustices in the Middle East, or your local church facing a season of transition. Or you could focus on a biblical truth you're trying to hold on to, like the fact that God is your provider and protector or that He promises to never leave you. Any way you want to see or hear or feel Jesus more clearly. You decide.

When we're fasting, every time we think of food, we can use it as a prompt to turn our thoughts back to our specific intention. As it turns out, we think about food so very many times a day. When I started fasting, I realized it was waaayyy more often than I would have guessed. And every time those food thoughts enter our minds, we can direct our thoughts back to an encouraging verse or prayer, back to Jesus.

Again, fasting is not a requirement. God doesn't tell us we have to fast. It's optional. If you believe in Jesus, you are already redeemed and forgiven, and there's a room waiting for you in heaven. And to be clear, there's also a fabulous feast prepared there. Fasting is not necessary, but for many of us it can be helpful.

What is your experience with fasting? What perceptions do you have of it—good or bad? Have you ever tried it? For health reasons? For physical reasons? For spiritual reasons? How did it go? I've talked to so many people about fasting, and they are all over the board with their opinions.

Fasting, for me, is hard. Good hard. Like a counseling appointment where my counselor digs deep, or a run on a day when my legs are tired. Afterward I'm always glad I did it. I'm better as a result. But I'm always grateful it's over. Fasting might be different for you, but that's how this practice is currently going in my life.

The first time I attempted a biblical fast, my first thought when I woke was, *Do we have any more of that yummy chocolate granola?* Then I remembered. *Oh yeah, I'm fasting today. Doesn't matter if we have it or not. Insert frowny face.*

When my daughter headed off to her morning soccer practice, I put cereal and grapes by her place to make sure she ate before she left. Without even thinking, I plucked a red grape from her bowl but then remembered I wasn't eating today and put it back. As I drove home from dropping off my son at a friend's, I wondered, *Hmm, do we have any chips left from Chipotle? Last night they were especially salty—my favorite.* Then I remembered even if we did, I wasn't going to eat them either. Later, I glanced at my watch and noticed it was almost noon. *Do we have any avocadoes I could slice to go with lunch?* I pictured the knife gliding through the smooth green flesh of the avocado and imagined the subtle taste and creaminess in my mouth.

Later my husband asked, "Hey, I'm running over to the farmers market. Do you want a cantaloupe or a watermelon?"

I could taste both, fresh, sweet, and juicy on my tongue, as he said the words.

"Either would be great," I answered meekly, trying to keep the conversation as short as possible.

With each thought of food—the granola, grapes, chips, avocado, and melons—I paused and reminded myself that I was fasting for a purpose. I spoke this verse over myself, "Man shall not live on bread alone, but on every word that comes from the mouth of God" (Matthew 4:4). Remember? In chapter 2, "Lighten Your Load," we talked about these words Jesus said to Satan in the wilderness when the devil was tempting Him. After reciting this verse, I thanked Jesus for His provision, because that's what

I had chosen to use this day of fasting to focus on: all the ways God provides for me.

We've talked about how fasting can help us focus on a biblical truth or prayer, but how else does limiting food intake for a set amount of time help us get closer to Jesus?

Fasting helps us be more aware of God's abundance.

For starters, fasting helps me be more aware of God's abundance.

All those zillion times a day when I think about food, I thank God that I am fortunate enough to have choices available not only to fill my belly but also to satisfy my whims. Our home has sweet blueberries, chocolate chips, and popsicles. We have salty popcorn, pretzels, and crackers. Even if I haven't been to the grocery in a while, I usually have the supplies to pour a bowl of cereal or boil a pot of pasta. And on days when I choose to fast, I am more acutely aware of this plenty. Because it's all there. If I needed it. And the only reason I have access to this food is because God has gifted it to me. It's all one-hundred-percent a gift. Thank you, Jesus!

Fasting also strengthens my "no button." It grows my self-control.

All those times I think of food on a fasting day, I tell myself, "No, because I've decided to fast today to get closer to Jesus." I remind myself that this is an intentional decision. I decide I will not eat lunch. I choose not to snack. I turn down a bite of someone's sandwich or cookie when they offer it to me. Not because I'm being good or following the rules, but because I really do want to get closer to Jesus. And all those noes create muscle memory.

163

That stronger "no muscle" comes in handy the next time I'm tempted to join in the gossip on the sidelines of my kid's game. I remind myself, "No, I won't say something snarky about that ref, coach, player, or person." Again, not because I'm good, not because those are the rules, but because I want to get closer to Jesus, and talking badly about others pulls me away from Him. That stronger self-control is helpful when my family is searching for a movie, and no one can agree, and someone finally suggests a film everyone says they'll watch—but when I pull up a review, I'm alerted there's a sex scene in it. I pull out my no again. Not because I've never seen a movie with a sex scene. Not because it's against the rules to watch such things. But because that movie does not portray sex as Jesus intended it, and letting my family view such a portrayal turns all of us a bit away from the ways of Jesus and a little toward the ways of culture.

Self-control is a fruit of the Holy Spirit living in every Christian. It's always there, but fasting fertilizes that fruit in me and helps it grow.

Fasting also helps me slow down.

So much of our lives revolves around instant gratification. I want to hear that song—I'll listen to it now on Spotify. I want to know that fact—I'll google it now. I want my mom's recipe for something—I'll text her. Why hasn't she responded? It's been two minutes!

Denying myself instant salty, savory, or sweet flavors when I fast heightens my awareness, so I pause and consider why I'm eating that, saying that, watching that, drinking that, picking up my phone . . . *before* I'm doing it. The hope is that these intentional pauses flow into my everyday non-fasting life.

Not to mention if you're skipping a meal, you get the time back you would have spent thinking about what to eat, preparing your meal, eating it, and cleaning up after yourself. By adding fasting in, you actually get some time back.

Fasting is a practice, not a performance; it's a time to build our faith, not perfect it.

If you fast, you'll probably fast differently than I do. Like the other spiritual disciplines, fasting is a choice to get closer to Jesus, not a rule we must follow. Also, it is a practice, not a performance. It's a time to build our faith, not perfect it. Personally, I fast once a month because I've found that's a good rhythm for me. I'm prone to fainting, so I plan out my fasting ahead of time, making sure I have what I need to stay safe. I eat a banana for breakfast. I have cold-pressed juices packed with nutrients in the fridge and drink one or two or three throughout the day if I feel dizzy. This makes sure my body functions properly while still feeling famished. I've already told you that I'm a runner and a walker. Fasting days are always walking days. I don't want to burn a crazy amount of calories and crash. In the evening, I eat dinner. And, wow, it tastes delicious.

I have a friend who fasts every week. She eats dinner the night before, drinks coffee in the morning, and then only drinks water until dinner. She and her husband fast together to support each other through the process. Another friend fasts when she has a big decision in front of her. She goes for two days without eating anything, only drinking water, but she might go five months or five years between fasts. Yet another friend removes certain food groups like sugar, dairy, and meat from her diet for a couple of weeks as her way to fast.

The point? To get closer to Jesus. That's it.

Fasting puts things in perspective for me. At the end of my fast, I notice the juiciness of a tomato and how queso fresco has a little salty something that makes it my favorite topping for street tacos. And if that is how one gal is satisfied by one simple meal after not eating for only one day, can you imagine how much more satisfying Jesus is? How He literally fills all our nooks and crannies, delights our senses, and leaves us wanting absolutely nothing? Because Jesus is our everything.

When our souls are hungry, we can go to Jesus. He will always satisfy. If you're hungry for attention, relief, healing, energy, purpose, justice, or friendship, you can be satisfied by our Savior, because He loves you fully, offers peace, is a healer, renews strength, calls you to good work, is a just God, and is the very best friend.

Fasting isn't the end all, and again, it's not by any means required to hang out with Jesus. But if you're looking for a way to appreciate Jesus's provision on a deeper level, if you'd like to grow your self-control, if there's a specific prayer you'd like to devote your attention to, I recommend you chat with God, chat with your doctor, and see if there's a way you can give fasting a try.

Because Jesus is the bread of life, and whoever comes to Him will never go hungry (John 6:35).

Slow Down

> Then Jesus declared, "I am the bread of life. Whoever comes to me will never go hungry, and whoever believes in me will never be thirsty." (John 6:35)

As you consider fasting, spend a few minutes talking to God about your body. Thank Him for creating you wonderfully and to inspire awe (Psalm 139:14). Thank Him for giving you feet that walk and hands that are holding this book and a nervous system and a digestive system and taste buds. Thank Him for making you in His image. And ask Him to let you fully believe these truths. That you are wonderfully made. That you are awe-inspiring. That you reflect the very image of the God of the universe. Ask Him to help you love the body He gave you.

If you'd like to give fasting a try, jot down a realistic plan of how you could integrate fasting into your life. You can start slowly. Fast from desserts for a week. Fast from snacks for two days. Skip one meal. Whatever works for you. Be intentional in the moments you would normally grab that dessert or snack or lunch and spend them in prayer.

If you're considering going a full day without eating, contact your doctor. If you're not due for an appointment, send your provider a message or call a nurse at your doctor's office to explain what you'd like to try and to get guidance. Once you have a plan and a medical professional's approval, pick a day and mark it on your calendar to try a fast.

CHAPTER 18

It's Just Practice

You Can Do It

We've talked about taking some things out of our lives and putting other things in. Through the pages of this book, we're trying to prioritize slowing down so we can

1. determine what really matters—what truly equates to a life worth living; and
2. once we've figured that out, actually savor the good stuff—the stuff life is made of.

But if you're zooming and skimming through the pages, it might feel like a lot. Clean out that closet. Put down your phone. Attempt a fast. Maybe you're not sure how you can do it all.

Interesting. Even this book is more effective when taken slowly. So, how's it going?

None of what we've talked about has meant to be an assignment. It's all meant to be an invitation to live more freely and to enhance your life. Some of these concepts might be things you've always done. Some might sound completely foreign to you. Most of them are countercultural. But we're not meant to perfect them.

We're just invited to figure out how we can work them into our day-to-day in ways that feel life-giving for us.

Slowing down, Sabbath, silence and solitude, prayer, and worship are all designed to help us understand God's heart. Because when we make time for these things, we better understand how much God loves us, that He desires goodness for us, and we're better able to live from a posture of this great love. These ways we've been trying to find rest and to refuel are sometimes referred to as spiritual practices or spiritual disciplines, but don't let those clunky words overwhelm you. The word *practice* is the key.

None of these approaches to slowing down and connecting with Jesus are mandates. They're not "must dos" or "thou shalts." They are simply avenues we can choose to seek God's heart. They are part of what Jesus calls "seeking first the kingdom of God" (see Matthew 6:33). Jesus tells us when we seek first God's kingdom, God "will give you everything you need" (NLT). Finding ways to slow down and incorporate Jesus into our lives is so worth it!

Living in this world, walking on this ground on the regular, sometimes makes it hard to remember that we have freedom today because Jesus says we do. That we are fully loved as we are. That there is joy available to us right now, no matter our circumstances. That we can find strength and endurance, not in ourselves but in the Lord God Almighty. That we can be hopeful when everything feels dark because Jesus is the light of the world.

Our culture will tell us otherwise. And so we forget. But when we take moments to be still, to clear out the clutter, and turn down the noise, it all becomes so clear. Like a fog is lifted. I want to cling to the clarity. But then a text will come through and the sink will leak and the oven timer will beep, and we rush to the next thing and the fog swirls back in.

We can't let this discourage us. The goal isn't to be perfect; it's to keep seeking.

The goal isn't to be perfect; it's to keep seeking.

Even in the midst of assignments, elections, and doctor appointments, we can seek first God's kingdom and grow our faith, strengthen our spirits, and boost our outlooks. We can go back to these practices again and again, even if everything looks different, even if we've stepped away from them for a while. These ways of seeking God first are always available to us. And it seems the more we do these things—declutter our minds, schedules, and feeds—the more we're able to tap into the love, joy, peace, patience, kindness, goodness, faithfulness, gentleness, and self-control that God has already put in us (Galatians 5:22–23).

I want all those things. So I keep practicing.

For all of us, it will be different. Being alone and quiet might make you fidgety. For me, it's restful. Fasting might be a game changer for your perspective. Or your doctor might tell you it's not safe for your body. You might pray in your cozy bed each morning before rising or on your back porch at night or while nursing your baby or driving your kids to school. Or you might pray better while walking the dog. Maybe you'll pause for ten seconds before typing that text, simply breathing and being still. Or maybe you'll pause every time you park, sitting in silence before getting out of your car.

There's not a right or wrong answer here, just a heart posture. A desire to get closer to Jesus. To know Him more so you can follow Him better. To talk to Him about everything. To stop when He tells you to stop and go when He tells you to go. To hand over your worries and traumas and struggles to Him. To listen to His voice. And then obey it. To seek first His kingdom.

We'll never master seeking God's kingdom first or understanding the heart of the God of the universe. No matter how long we're at it. Because the ways of the Lord are too multifaceted for us humans to master. But we can practice. We can try to figure out how to slow down and seek Jesus in ways that work in our specific lives. Each time we practice, we take a step closer to God and all the goodness He has for us.

Second Kings 5 tells of a king's commander named Naaman, who had leprosy and was miraculously healed by God's power through the prophet Elisha. Naaman was forever changed. Although he came from a culture where people worshipped multiple gods, Naaman discovered there was only one true God—Yahweh, the LORD God of Israel, who healed him. And Naaman wanted to figure out a way to seek Yahweh first even when he returned home to his pagan culture.

Once healed, Naaman made a peculiar request to Elisha: "Please allow me to load two of my mules with earth from this place, and I will take it back home with me" (v. 17 NLT). What in the actual world does Naaman want with sacks of dirt? What does this have to do with us and our seeking God's kingdom?

Naaman had to get creative to find a way he could seek God in his specific situation. He thought about it, and he made it work. Naaman was a king's officer and had to return to his land and his job. Naaman's way of staying faithful and focused on seeking God was carrying back some dirt from Israel. When others would bow down to false gods, Naaman sprinkled dirt on the ground and knelt in that dirt, a physical, gritty, earthy reminder of how God had transformed him inside and out.[1] I imagine every time Naaman spread a little dirt on the ground, he first held up a handful to his nose, recalling the scents of Israel. People might have asked him what in the world he was doing. But I picture Naaman letting the soil slowly trickle through his fingers, noticing how healed his once-leprous skin now was. Naaman was being intentional in his own, creative, quirky way.

We can too. That's really what this book is all about—intentionally seeking and following Jesus. And figuring out ways that work for us in our situations, locations, and stages of life.

You and I probably won't, and probably shouldn't, sprinkle dirt from Israel in our closets or on our office floors, but we can figure out ways to make Jesus the priority in our lives. We'll have to slow down some. We'll have to give up some things. We'll have to say no to some things. We'll have to be okay with going against the grain. But the fruit available to us is bountiful.

We'll find ourselves more at peace because we've downloaded our worries to Jesus. We'll find ourselves more content because we'll be more aware of how much Jesus gives and satisfies us. We'll find ourselves being more patient because we're less stressed, kinder, and more aware of how much God does for us. We'll more frequently tap into the power of the Holy Spirit placed inside believers. We'll feel more joyful because we'll be more aware of God's goodness, thanking Him for it and celebrating all He's doing in our lives.

It will take practice to make these new rhythms feel natural.

But it will take practice to make these new rhythms feel natural. When I was growing up, people would notice I had long fingers and ask, "Do you play piano?" Or they'd say, "You should play piano." It saddened me when I always answered no. Was I missing out on something? I loved the sound of the instrument, and the idea of playing piano seemed romantic. When I was in sixth grade, my mom received a small inheritance from an aunt and bought a piano with it. Mom had played as a girl and always wanted one in our house. This was my chance.

But despite my long fingers, playing piano took practice. I didn't sit down at my first lesson and play my favorite song. There were weeks and weeks of worksheets, learning how to read music, and playing scales. As time went on, I graduated to simple songs like "Hot Cross Buns" and "Lavender's Blue." But it was months before I played a song I hadn't sung in preschool, and those were still simplified versions of pop songs my teacher transposed for me. Still, it was a thrill. And always, no matter how long I played or how I progressed, there were finger exercises: repetitive, rapid practices to teach my fingers how to fly across the keyboard, how to cross over one another without getting tangled, how to find the right keys at the right time.

There were weeks where I practiced every day with fervor. When my piano teacher, Miss Julie, returned the following Tuesday, I confidently played what she'd asked me to practice. She'd assign me more of a song I liked or, if I was lucky, a new one.

But there were also weeks when it hit me Tuesday after school that Miss Julie would be coming in an hour, and I hadn't practiced a note. These weeks I was not getting any closer to mastering the piano. I tried to cram in a week's worth of practice into one hour, hoping she wouldn't be able to tell. Although Miss Julie never got angry with me, she could always tell. So could I. I'd miss notes or mess up the timing of a lively tarantella.

I couldn't fake it, because when we don't practice, we don't get better. It's the same with our spiritual practices. Like Miss Julie, God won't get mad if we don't practice. Our God is compassionate and gracious, slow to anger, and abounding in love and faithfulness (Exodus 34:6). He'll never punish us for not practicing this week, month, or season. But our good and gracious God will always show up when we're willing to slow down and spend time with Him. And it's in the practice that we become progressively more in tune with God's love and joy and grace.

We have our entire lives to seek ways to slow down, be still, and listen to God's loving voice.

These habits of slowing down we're trying to incorporate into our lives are called practices because we never perfect them. Thankfully, we never have to. We never have the performance or recital or game where all the practice needs to pay off. We have our entire lives to seek ways to slow down, be still, and listen to God's loving voice. We don't have to work more or try harder; we just benefit when we consistently show up.

It's simply about trusting Jesus. About saying, "Okay, I'll give this up for you. I'll put this down for you. I'll devote this time to you." Then letting Him do all the work of showering grace and kindness on us. The goal is simply to get closer to Jesus. To seek ways to be *with Jesus* and let Him do what He likes to do—love us perfectly. It is this beautiful time together that Jesus can use to refine, guide, strengthen, calm, grow, refresh, and love us.

We'll have seasons where we're one-hundred-percent all in and seasons where we fall out of practice. Some of these practices we'll look forward to. Others we'll continue to try or adjust until we find our own personal bag of dirt, because we know when we do, we're better for it. Some of these practices we might not be ready to try yet. And the beauty of all these opportunities is we can always come back to them, sprinkle our proverbial soil on the ground, feel it, and smell it, and Jesus will be waiting to grow all kinds of goodness in us, to calm and restore us.

When I sit down at the piano today, all these years later, my fingers usually feel a little rusty. It takes a few minutes to remember the cadence of a song I used to play. But I can always slide onto that bench, follow the notes on the paper, and play a familiar melody. The same is true with our faith journeys. Any time, day or night, we can pray, pause, go off by ourselves, worship, fast, or pick up our Bibles; Jesus is waiting to play the sweetest love song for us we've ever heard.

Slow Down

> But seek first his kingdom and his righteousness, and all these things will be given to you as well. (Matthew 6:33)

Which of the practices are you enjoying the most so far?

Which are you struggling with?

Commit today to devote some time to Jesus. You choose how. Ask Him to grow your love, joy, peace, patience, kindness, goodness, faithfulness, gentleness, and self-control during your time together.

CHAPTER 19

Charcuterie To Go

Savor the Flavor

I was sitting in our car in the parking lot of the high school, as I've found myself doing every summer for years. Our kids' school is fortunate enough to have a weight room and an experienced and motivated trainer who requires all athletes to report to the weight room once or twice a week all summer long for injury-prevention purposes. Which is wonderful. However, the school is twenty-five minutes from our house, and the lifting sessions for each team last half an hour. Going back home isn't an option. Sometimes I call a friend or bring my laptop to get a little work done or take a short walk down the sidewalk. Today it is ninety-four degrees, and I just turned in an article. I'm working on living out this book when possible, so I brought a paperback and my lunch to simply slow down.

Last night my husband was at a fundraiser catered by a company that specializes in charcuterie. They created charcuterie cones. Think of a paper snow cone, but instead of being filled with shaved ice and sweet cherry syrup, it's filled with small skewers of chewy, fresh mozzarella balls, tangy olives, and bright cherry tomatoes.

Tiny wedges of sharp cheese, wrinkly dried apricots, miniature wheels of salami, and crunchy corn nuts were sprinkled in as well.

My son went inside to lift with his cross-country team. I slid my seat back, cracked open my novel, and pulled a bite of mozzarella off the stick with my teeth. It was so creamy and melted in my mouth. Yum! Next, I picked up an apricot that had some corn nuts stuck to its sticky surface. Instead of popping the whole thing in my mouth, I nibbled off a tiny bite. So sweet. And the salty crunch of the corn nut was a surprisingly delicious complement. I took a sip of water, cool from my aluminum bottle, and read a few pages of my book. Next, I tugged a rolled-up piece of salami off the stick. The smoky, spicy flavor exploded in my mouth. I've eaten dried apricots, salami, and fresh mozzarella many times before, but today I was really tasting this food, savoring it, not wolfing it down or shoving it in my mouth.

As I sat there amazed at this little cone of deliciousness, I realized I'd eaten my last three meals—maybe more—standing up. For breakfast, I'd eaten a bite of oatmeal, then turned on the coffee machine. Then spooned in another couple of bites before tossing in a load of laundry. Then one last giant bite before placing vitamins at each family member's place at the kitchen table. Last night's dinner had been leftover pizza I heated up in the microwave as I scurried around the house organizing things before heading out the door. Yeah, same for lunch yesterday. We're in a busy season before school starts but fall sports have already begun. There are so many things to sign and print and volunteer for, and supplies and pieces of equipment and snacks I need to make sure we have on hand. I'm grateful for all of it. For hot, sunny August days, and the sports my kids enjoy, and the ability and privilege that they're able to participate. But somehow eating has simply become a way to fuel my body instead of a way to savor all the delicious foods and flavors God has created.

As Anne Lamott says, "For something to be delicious, you have to be present to savor it."[1]

Are you a sit-down-and-enjoy-a-meal person?

Or have you been eating on the go?

Yes, there are times we need to eat and run, but Jesus invites us to s-l-o-w down and enjoy a good meal. Jesus was a busy man. He was on mission. He knew He had three years to train up His disciples and teach the people about God's love, grace, freedom, and joy. He had throngs of people coming up to Him on the streets, asking to be healed. Yet, throughout the Gospels, we see Jesus taking time to sit and eat.

> While Jesus was having dinner at Matthew's house, many tax collectors and sinners came and ate with him and his disciples. (Matthew 9:10)

> When he was at the table with them, he took bread, gave thanks, broke it and began to give it to them. (Luke 24:30)

> The apostles gathered around Jesus and reported to him all they had done and taught. Then, because so many people were coming and going that they did not even have a chance to eat, he said to them, "Come with me by yourselves to a quiet place and get some rest." (Mark 6:30–31)

This last passage always screams at me. Because there are days when I don't feel like I have time to eat. You? It's nice to know we're not alone. The disciples were also so busy coming and going that they didn't have time to eat. Jesus recognized this was their situation. And He recognizes it might be ours too. Jesus isn't saying, "Shame on you. I can't believe you aren't enjoying the good food I made for you." But He is saying, "Hey, I see you. You've been doing good work. Thank you for caring for the people and tasks I've given you. But if you haven't had time to eat, that's a sign that you need to take a break. Slow down and rest. Come away with me."

Jesus invites us into moments of rest in the midst of the busy.

He's inviting us into moments of rest in the midst of the busy.

We need food to live, but God is so loving that He didn't just invent hardtack, those gross cracker things sailors and Civil War soldiers relied on because they lasted *forever*. And God didn't just create IVs for us to get all our nutrients through a tube. Those things have a time and place, and how cool that God nudged some humans to invent them for their specific purposes. But God wants us to enjoy food. He created sweet, juicy pineapple, peppery arugula, fiery habanero peppers, and multitudes of spices and herbs to flavor our food. God gave humankind creativity and intellect to invent ovens and grills and recipes that turn grain into flour and flour into pastas or pastries.

Sadly, we often sprint through our meals, barely tasting them. Maybe you're wonderful at sitting down and slowly enjoying everything you eat. If so, you're amazing. I'm trying to be more like you. But I know I'm not alone here. Research from the Institute of Food Technologists shows 46 percent of meals are eaten alone.[2] And that trend has been on the rise for the last thirty years. We eat in our cars or on public transport as we get from here to there. We eat at our kids' games and throw a few bites in our mouths between meetings or at our desks while we work. And as we're multitasking with our morsels and mouthfuls, we're missing out on the gift of food.

As we're multitasking with our morsels and mouthfuls, we're missing out on the gift of food.

Taste and see that the Lord is good;
   blessed is the one who takes refuge in him.
                                        (Psalm 34:8)

Taste is one of the five senses God blessed us with. We can taste and see some of His goodness when we eat, but also when we drink. Do you even know what you drank today or how much of it or when you drank it or how long you made each beverage last? Did you let the fizz of bubbles dance on your tongue, or allow your tea to warm you on a chilly day?

God was the editor of the Bible. There are so many details God left out because He didn't think we needed to know them, but I'm still curious. What were they wearing? How much time passed between those two interactions? I know that's what she *said*, but what was she *thinking*? This makes me pay attention to the details God intentionally left in. And over and over again in the Gospels, we see stories of Jesus eating as important details God wanted us to read and know about. "When one of the Pharisees invited Jesus to have dinner with him, he went to the Pharisee's house and reclined at the table" (Luke 7:36).

Jesus "reclined" at the table, eating with His friends. Can you picture Him? Leaning back after dinner? Arm outstretched over the person next to Him, showing love and attention to whoever sat there? That's not a picture of someone who wants us to shove down their food between activities.

In the movie *Paris Can Wait*, Diane Lane plays Anne, the wife of a movie producer. The film begins with the couple in Cannes, France, headed to Paris. Suddenly the husband's hectic filming schedule demands that he take a side trip to Budapest. Her husband's business partner, Jacques, offers to drive Anne to Paris, where she'll meet her husband after his day trip to Hungary.

But Jacques moves at a different pace than Anne is accustomed to. He stops every hour to stretch his legs. He pulls off the road to explore Roman ruins and takes the long way to drive past lavender fields in bloom. Jacques is not a drive-through kind of guy. He plans their route to include some of his favorite restaurants, ordering exquisite dishes, multiple courses paired with wines, and at least four chocolate desserts. Jacques picks wild watercress from a field and invites Anne to taste it then and there, fresh from the ground. Jacques savors life.

Do we understand how slowing down to taste and see the goodness of God can play out?

Or are we so focused on getting from here to there that we aren't tasting the apricots or the watercress? That we're forgetting to taste and see that the Lord is good—so very, very good?

Let's take a hint from Jesus. Let's recline, break bread, and seek the Lord's goodness.

Slow Down

> Taste and see that the LORD is good;
>> blessed is the one who takes refuge in him.
> Fear the LORD, you his holy people,
>> for those who fear him lack nothing.

The lions may grow weak and hungry,
>but those who seek the LORD lack no good thing.
>(Psalm 34:8–10)

When was the last time you truly savored a meal?

Slow down and take time to plan out a delectable dinner, a playful picnic in the park, or a bountiful brunch. You can make a grocery list and schedule time in the kitchen or make a reservation or order carryout. You choose what feeds your soul.

Invite someone to join you. Allow yourself to sip and nibble instead of gulp. Notice the textures and tastes. Talk about them with your companion. Maybe even challenge each other to both bring something new to the meal that neither of you have tried before.

Take time to thank God for His goodness!

CHAPTER 20

Magic Spot
Getting Outside

My mom is a retired schoolteacher who volunteers one day a week at a nature center, leading field trips for elementary students. I wish you could see her explaining the lesson she teaches about pollination and how she makes all the students scurry here and there like bees from this to that plant. Or that you could see her hazel eyes light up when she explains how pure and sweet and perfect the syrup is during their maple-syruping adventures in the cold of winter. All of it sounds like a blast to me, but when I asked Mom what the students' favorite activity was, she said without hesitation, "Magic Spot."

"What's that?" I asked.

"It's when I take the kids to this little part of the woods and have them all find a peaceful spot to sit for twenty-five minutes in silence. They're allowed to sit wherever they want in that area, but they have to sit alone and apart from everyone else. And they can't make a noise. At first they groan, 'Twenty-five minutes!'" She mimics a whiny kid's voice, then continues. "The kids fidget. But then you see them relaxing and just sitting. They're always disappointed when the time is up. The kids who come back later in the year always ask when they can do Magic Spot."

My husband is a college professor and does something similar with the students in his Faith and Entrepreneurship class. He makes them leave their phones in the classroom, which causes some of the college kids to break into a cold sweat. Then Brett instructs them to find a quiet place to sit for half an hour. They have to be by themselves. They have to go outside. At the end of the semester on their comment cards, this activity is always the fan favorite of his students, hands down.

Why?

Why does a gaggle of grade-schoolers who struggle to sit still for six minutes look forward to returning to their Magic Spot? Why does a class of college students who panic without their smartphones find this to be their favorite activity of the term?

We already talked about some of the benefits of silence in the "Quiet Time" chapter. But being outside while being quiet is something especially sweet. Being quiet with nature is something humans crave. It's good for us. Being outside increases our vitamin D levels, lowers our stress and blood pressure, decreases our anxiety and depression, increases our concentration, and can even help us sleep better.[1] Pretty amazing. Pair that with silencing some of the noise in our world and we have a dynamic duo.

Getting into God's creation is nurturing to our bodies, minds, and souls.

Getting into God's creation is nurturing to our bodies, minds, and souls. Trouble is, we're so busy running here and there, making one more phone call and putting away one more dish and doing one more sit-up in our climate-controlled, artificially lit homes, schools, and workplaces, that we sometimes don't realize we haven't been outside in hours or even days. Our brains are overloaded with constant images and sounds and blue lights. It's not uncommon for people to turn on the TV because the sound helps them fall asleep or to keep their phones in their beds, where buzzes and pings disturb their sleep. I can't think of a single shop, store, or restaurant that doesn't have music playing. I love music. But our souls long to take a break from the constant noise and manufactured environments so we can exhale.

Being quiet outside isn't something my mom or husband made up—although I applaud them for exposing their students to it—God did. When He created the earth, God didn't put humankind in a building with a soundtrack but in a garden. "Now the LORD God had planted a garden in the east, in Eden; and there he put the man he had formed. The LORD God made all kinds of trees grow out of the ground—trees that were pleasing to the eye and good for food" (Genesis 2:8–9).

I'm sure Adam and Eve chatted with each other. But probably not all the time. I'm guessing they also worked in silence sometimes. Maybe Adam wandered off to check on some animals over here while Eve was taking care of the plants over there. God plopped humankind smack in the middle of a beautiful garden full of trees. Makes sense that our hearts would long to get back to the place where we came from. Going outside reminds us of God's glory.

> The heavens declare the glory of God;
> the skies proclaim the work of his hands. . . .

> In the heavens God has pitched a tent for the sun.
>> It is like a bridegroom coming out of his chamber,
>> like a champion rejoicing to run his course.
> It rises at one end of the heavens
>> and makes its circuit to the other;
>> nothing is deprived of its warmth.
>
> (Psalm 19:1, 4–6)

It's all glorious. The daily circuit of the sun. Pastel sunrises smudged with peach and purple. Stars suspended in the sky, trillions of miles away. The pale glow of the moon, changing shape throughout the month. And it's quiet. Yes, there is the song of crickets, the rustle of leaves, and the whoosh of the wind, but what peaceful, restorative sounds. Slowing down to soak in the outdoors reminds us of how great our God is. How powerful He is to create all these things. How caring He is to make them so beautiful and unique. How brilliant He is to have invented sunlight to work and play by and starlight to snooze under—day and night, a built-in timer on the outdoor lights, another perfect rhythm.

We can lose sight of who God is or doubt what He can do.

When we're pulled in every direction by toddlers literally tugging on our legs or clients vying for our time or commitments running us ragged, we can lose sight of who God is or doubt what He can do. Intentionally slowing down for a minute or thirty outside reminds us of how brilliant God is, helps this truth sink into our souls.

When Job lost his family, possessions, and health and felt at his most desolate, God reminded Job of who He was by detailing how He created nature. Take a moment to actually read through this passage.

> Have you entered the storehouses of the snow
> > or seen the storehouses of the hail,
> which I reserve for times of trouble,
> > for days of war and battle?
> What is the way to the place where the lightning is
> > > dispersed,
> > or the place where the east winds are scattered
> > > over the earth?
> Who cuts a channel for the torrents of rain,
> > and a path for the thunderstorm . . . ?
>
> Can you bind the chains of the Pleiades?
> > Can you loosen Orion's belt?
> Can you bring forth the constellations in their seasons
> > or lead out the Bear with its cubs? . . .
>
> Can you raise your voice to the clouds
> > and cover yourself with a flood of water?
> Do you send the lightning bolts on their way?
> > Do they report to you, "Here we are"? . . .
> Who has the wisdom to count the clouds?
> > Who can tip over the water jars of the heavens?
> > > (Job 38:22–25, 31–32, 34–35, 37)

This chapter gets me every time.

If you've seen snow, hail, wind, grass, lightning, or the Big Dipper, then you've seen God at work. We humans aren't capable of making any of those things. Not one of them. But God created them all. And when we get out in nature, we remember. We marvel. Because what God has made is marvelous. Because the Maker of all this wonder and beauty—all these elements and creatures—He is the most marvelous.

Remembering that this is who our God is settles our worries into place. It reframes our concerns, because if the One who "marked off the dimensions" (v. 5) of the earth is in charge and on our side, He can probably make sure we have enough time to get to the things that matter most. The one who orders around the lightning bolts has the capacity to tackle the problem we're spinning our wheels over. Getting outside, out of our hurry, reminds us we're going to be okay. If He gives ants the capability to carry up to twenty times their body weight and rabbits the power to hop nine feet in a single bound, don't you think our God can equip you for whatever you're facing? Help you jump through the hurdles and carry the weight on your shoulders?

How often do you get outside? You don't have to go on a field trip to make it happen. You can even do this if you live in a city.

You could sit on your porch or rooftop tonight and stare at the stars or the sliver of moon shining in the sky. You could step out of your office building and walk somewhere to lunch or eat outside on a bench. You could take a slow lap around the parking lot on your break to ask God how to handle a situation at work. You could go for a bike ride without your headphones, allowing the wind to blow through your hair as you unpack what's on your mind with Jesus.

Thank God for today, and ask for His guidance throughout this day.

Or on a day when you can't imagine how you'll find any time outside, step out your front door first thing, before you touch your phone in the morning, or open a window and pop your head out. Fill your lungs with a giant gulp of fresh air. Notice the temperature. How it smells outside. Listen for a moment. Thank God for today, and ask for His guidance throughout this day.

You can move your body outside—everything from a walk to jumping rope to spreading out your Pilates mat in your yard or a nearby park. You can go outside in the morning or at teatime or take an after-dinner walk around the block and make it a new ritual. If you're the one in charge, why not hold a meeting or class in the courtyard or on the lawn? Going outside and reconnecting to God's creation, reminding yourself of who He is and what He is capable of, can be a consistent, recalibrating rhythm in our lives.

We need this.

You may not know it yet, but a Magic Spot awaits you. One where you exhale. One where you lay your worries at Jesus's feet. One where you gain clarity on a big decision or peace around the thing you're stressed about. One where your busy body and brain can rest. One where you notice the smell of honeysuckle or the whirr of grasshoppers rubbing their legs together or how silent it is when it snows. Maybe you'll go barefoot and savor the feel of sand or grass between your toes. Maybe giant clouds or mountains will remind you of how big and grand our God must be. Perhaps a delicate spiderweb will illustrate how detail-oriented and intricate our God is. Or watching a bee buzz amongst the flowers, both pollinating those flowers and gathering the ingredients to produce sweet, sticky honey you can slather on fresh baked biscuits might blow your mind and reassure you that God knows how to get things done in ways you could never imagine.

Wherever your Magic Spot is, you'll find that there, outdoors in the quiet, you can reconnect to who God created you to be, to how much He loves you, to the very world He created for us to live in. And you'll find yourself wondering when you can return.

Slow Down

> The heavens declare the glory of God;
>> the skies proclaim the work of his hands.
>>> (Psalm 19:1)

Do you have a Magic Spot—a place outside where you get away by yourself? If so, describe it. How often do you go there?

If not, scout one out today. Where could you go?

Head outside for ten minutes. If it's rainy, grab an umbrella or sit under a shelter. If it's cold, slip on a coat. Your schedule jammed? Schedule it for tomorrow.

While you're there, consider taking your Bible and reading Job 38 in its entirety, marveling at our Creator and His creation.

How did you feel when you were outside? What did God do for your soul?

CHAPTER 21

Thank-You Notes

Gratitude

A group of six of us gathers every few weeks. You can use the term "small group" or "life group" or "house church" or "community group" or whatever you like, but really we just look forward to getting together and talking about Jesus and how He's working in our lives. One evening in early fall, sitting on our back porch, I listened to my friends share honestly about what they'd been distracted by lately. Eventually Beth asked me, "Laura, you've been quiet. What about you?"

"I didn't know when we started tonight," I began. "But as I'm listening and processing, I realize I'm distracted by trying to protect my kids. So, sort of like Brenda shared, I'm trying to control the outcomes for them." I looked down and then back up to the kind faces gathered around our table, illuminated by the twinkling fairy lights I'd set in glass jars as centerpieces. "We moved Max into a house on campus with friends a few weeks ago. Then we moved Mallory off to college the following week. Then Maguire got his driver's license last week and is driving himself places. This all happened in three weeks! And honestly, I don't think I've had time to process any of it, because we've gone from one big life change to the next." Somewhere along my confession, my voice cracked and my eyes brimmed with tears.

"I just love them so much, and I can't protect them anymore," I continued. "I can't keep Maguire safe while he's driving. I want to, but I can't. And I'm not able to keep Mallory from catty girls or guys with poor intentions at college. I can't make sure Max takes care of himself or manages his time well." It all sounded silly as it poured out of me, but it was real, a heart's cry I hadn't even known was in me.

My friends were sympathetic. "That's a lot," Brenda said, nodding.

Our friend Andrea from Italy was staying with us, so of course he was invited around our table that night. He looked at me and said, "I know you trust God. It is time to trust God to protect your kids and guide them. You know He loves your children. You can open up your hands, like this"—Andrea turned his palms upward—"and trust them in God's care."

Andrea's words rang true. I did know that God loves my kiddos more than I do. That He had protected them in the past. That I could trust Him to guide my children. This was logical. And I believed it. I told other people this about their kids all the time. But my mama heart wanted to shield my kids from the pain and tragedy of this broken world. Wrap them in bubble wrap. I knew in my head I could trust God, but my heart hadn't caught up to that truth. There had been a time when our kiddos were small when I was responsible for so much—almost everything. Now it was a new season where they needed me less. I was so used to being their provider and protector, but I never truly was doing it by myself. I was working with God, and of course Brett, to raise these kids. Now it was time to release even more of them into God's hands, though my instinct was to hold them tightly in mine.

How did I combat that?

The answer wasn't on the tip of my tongue that night, but it was forming as Andrea spoke, as I spoke to myself an affirmation that God *had* provided and protected my kids. That I could trust Him. In the morning, I armed myself with my Bible, coffee, and journal, and Jesus helped me figure it out.

Remember how I've protected them, He nudged me.

And so I pulled out my lime-green pen and started writing down all the ways God had provided for and protected my kiddos in the past couple of weeks, since my emotional roller coaster began. The list was specific and long. It ranged from God guiding Mallory to the college where she was enrolled and giving her two Christian roommates to an award Maguire received from his coaches, recognizing his hard work in cross-country. It included the Friday morning worship times Max and his housemates hosted each week and the fact that God had given our oldest, Maddie, a job that used her giftings so well to help others while also bringing her joy. These were all things I had zero control of or part in. All beautiful ways God encouraged, protected, guided, and inspired my kids. His kids.

What's distracting you from the peace, love, joy, and abundance God has for you?

What are you trying to control? What are you holding on to too tightly and it's stressing you out? What's distracting you from the peace, love, joy, and abundance God has for you?

Maybe you're having work done on your house and you can't

control the contractors or the costs. You're spending precious hours every day after they leave surveying their work, making sure surfaces are level and cracks are caulked. Maybe your toddler is throwing tantrums, and even though you're applying all the parenting tips you have up your sleeve, your child still melts down every night. So you listen to another podcast and read another parenting book late into the evening. Or maybe you're worried about a friend who has an addiction. You're checking in on them, suggesting they get help, researching support groups, but they won't take the first step.

"My grace is sufficient for you, for my power is made perfect in weakness." (2 Corinthians 12:9)

There's nothing wrong with making sure things are going smoothly, learning the best practices of parenting, or caring for a struggling friend. Those are actually all noble pursuits. But when we keep trying to fix, heal, control, protect, and make everyone happy, we can wear ourselves out. Turns out it's not all up to us. Thankfully. As the Lord told the apostle Paul, "My grace is sufficient for you, for my power is made perfect in weakness" (2 Corinthians 12:9).

One way to remember this truth is by slowing down enough to thank God for what He's already done through His grace and His power.

As I journaled that morning, Christ's peace that surpasses all understanding flooded me. Because this is what gratitude does.

It turns us away from worry and toward appreciation. It turns off our concerns that something will go awry if we don't handle everything correctly and turns on the realization that God is the one in control. It frees up space in our crowded mind so we can stop scheming how to fix all these things and instead hand them over to God. And that is a very good thing.

Paul instructed the church in Philippi to use prayers of thanksgiving to ward off worry. I'm here to tell you it works. "Do not be anxious about anything, but in every situation, by prayer and petition, with thanksgiving, present your requests to God" (Philippians 4:6).

It's a simple exercise—gratitude. It's simple because you don't need to have any training or special resources. And as with anything we practice, the more we do it, the better we become.

This morning I am grateful for rain watering the mums I bought from Maguire's cross-country team's fundraiser. They're still sitting in their pots in our yard where we unloaded them from the car. Since I hadn't found time to tend to the flowers yet, God provided water for their roots. He's good like that. I'm also thankful for a shot of espresso, rich and bold, waking up my senses. I'm grateful that Maguire made it safely to school this morning—that God protected our boy during his drive. I'm thankful for a zinnia seed I planted back in May, which has since sprouted and grown and is beginning to unfurl its orange petals, on the verge of exploding into a vibrant, fiery bloom. I'm thankful for the scent of the lavender-vanilla candle I lit this morning and the peaceful mood it sets for me as I type while the rain patters on the windows outside.

Simple.

And as I type this list, I think, *Oh yeah, I'm also grateful for this super soft red plaid blanket draped across my lap, and the crimson cardinals perched on our bird feeder.* You see what I mean. Once you start thanking God for things, it's hard to stop. Because our

God is so good, His giving to us so lavish, we should sing as the old hymn "Blessed Assurance" declares, "This is my story, this is my song, praising my Savior all the day long."

Once you start thanking God for things, it's hard to stop. Our God is so good, His giving to us is so lavish.

One of the many lessons I wanted to instill in my kiddos while they were still under my care was the importance of writing thank-you notes. When they were little, I'd have them draw a picture of the book an aunt or uncle gave them for their birthday or the Lego set they received for Christmas. I'd write the words, "Thank you so much for my . . ." and insert the picture my child drew. "I love you," I'd add, and then have my child sign their name if they could. As they got older, they wrote actual notes, and eventually they addressed and stamped the envelopes and placed them in the mailbox themselves.

This instilling of writing thank-you notes mattered because, first, it's good manners. If someone took the time to select something for us and make sure it got to us, we should acknowledge and thank them. Second, this act of gratitude makes us slow down and appreciate the gift more. It makes us pause and consider what we like about it and how loved we are that someone would do this for us. Third, gratitude is good for our souls, for our joy quotient. When we immerse ourselves in gratitude for what we do have, it helps us be present and makes our longings for what we wish we had less acute.

I taught my kids to write thank-you notes to people, but it's even more important to thank Jesus. Because as James (Jesus's brother) tells us, "Every good and perfect gift is from above, coming down from the Father of the heavenly lights, who does not change like shifting shadows" (James 1:17).

Jesus Himself modeled how we can write these thank-you notes to God when He gives us a little or a lot of something. Jesus gave thanks when there was just a little bit of food to feed a giant crowd (Matthew 15:36). And after He gave thanks, those seven little loaves and a few fish fed thousands, with seven baskets of leftovers (v. 37).

Jesus thanked the Father *before* Lazarus came out of his grave (John 11:41). Thanking God in advance for what was going to happen. Trusting God to pull through for Him.

Jesus gave thanks to God for bread and wine (Luke 22:17–19). They were physical sustenance and symbols both of God protecting the Israelites from Pharaoh at the first Passover and of what Jesus was about to do on the cross.

Every single day, we can thank Jesus for breaking His body and pouring out His blood for us.

We can thank God for being with us, for listening, and for performing the miracles He performs. We can be grateful for things we can see and things we cannot see, for ways God has been there in the past and things He is doing for us right now.

And every single day, we can thank Jesus for breaking His body and pouring out His blood for us.

Look around you right now. What can you thank Jesus for? You don't even have to get up from your seat. How about taking something you're concerned about and finding ways to praise God for how He's moved before in that area? For example, if you're worried about work, what is one positive about your current job? A paycheck? A short commute? Your desk mate? What is one way God has previously provided for you with your work? Has He orchestrated an introduction or interview that you couldn't have managed on your own? Trained you with a skill you ended up needing later?

We can flip our worries and concerns and frustrations into joy and satisfaction simply by jotting a quick thank-you note to Jesus.

If you were sitting around a table of friends, you'd probably have some worries and concerns of your own you'd like to share. Some things lingering on the outskirts of your mind, distracting you from God's goodness. If so, I urge you to confide in your special people and ask them for prayer. And as an antidote to those distractions, I encourage you to practice gratitude.

Slow Down

> Give thanks in all circumstances; for this is God's will for you in Christ Jesus. (1 Thessalonians 5:18)

Jot down anything you're currently feeling stressed about.

Now, write a thank-you note to Jesus. To warm up your gratitude muscles and get started, thank God for one thing you can see, one thing you can touch, one thing you can taste, one thing you can hear, and one thing you can smell.

Consider the concern you jotted down. What can you praise God for around this specific situation? It can be something big or something small.

CHAPTER 22

Cymbals and Drumsticks

Celebration

We were at 2.9 out of 3.1 miles on a Thanksgiving morning 5K Turkey Trot when I saw the women handing out drumsticks. No, not turkey drumsticks but wooden drumsticks, like a drummer uses to play drums.

It was chilly—coats-and-gloves chilly. But that's what Thanksgiving looks like in Ohio. Luckily, we were wearing goofy brown knit hats with turkey faces stitched on the front and "Wobble 'til you gobble" stitched on the back to keep us warm.

I don't think my daughter or mom who were walking with me even noticed the drumsticks. My girl had spied one of her favorite high school teachers, and they were busy chatting as we walked along the route. My mom, who had come in second in her age group the prior year, was laser focused on her speed, aiming for first this year. The rest of our family had run instead of walked and were already across the finish line at the cupcake tent. But in front of me was a smiling woman's outstretched hand, holding a drumstick. And right beyond her were cymbals on stands. As people passed, they could triumphantly clang the cymbals with their stick as a way to say, "Look, I made it this far! I'm going to finish! I'm doing it! Woo-hoo!"

So I grabbed a stick, solid in my hand, thanked the woman, and clanged all three cymbals as I passed, their brassy chimes loud and invigorating. As their sound echoed through the air, it struck me that these ladies took their Thanksgiving morning to set up a creative, fun, sensory way for others to celebrate. How awesome is that?

How often do you celebrate?

Every amazing or wonderful thing we experience happens because God cleared the way, put things in motion, and made it so.

Every amazing or wonderful thing we experience happens because God cleared the way, put things in motion, and made it so. Celebrating His goodness, faithfulness, and abundance is a very good idea. In fact, it's biblical. When God gave Moses the Ten Commandments plus a slew of other regulations on how to best live life, God mandated festivals.

Yup. God created celebrations and insisted His people have them (Leviticus 23:2). Every year they were to celebrate the Passover, the Feast of Booths, the Feast of Weeks (a harvest celebration), the Feast of First Fruits, the Feast of Trumpets, and the Day of Atonement. These were times set apart to put down work, gather, feast, refuel, and give thanks because the Lord is good!

In Esther 9, there is much ado about the festival of Purim, which celebrates how Queen Esther stopped the genocide of the Jews (so worth celebrating!). The Bible tells us this wasn't a one-and-done deal. Verse 28 says, "These days should be remembered and observed in every generation by every family, and in every province and in every city. And these days of Purim should never fail to be celebrated by the Jews—nor should the memory of these days die out among their descendants." This festival should never fail to be celebrated. By any Jewish family. Ever. My Jewish friends still celebrate Purim today.

Jesus's first miracle was at a wedding celebration, and one of His most profound sermons was during the Festival of Booths (also known as the Festival of Tabernacles) in John 7.

God is serious about celebrations.

God is serious about celebrations. He wants us to pause, put down our work, recall and proclaim how good He is—what He has accomplished through us—and revel in it.

When was the last time you celebrated?

And let's think about those celebrations. Did they feel like a lot of work? Were they out of habit? Or did you actually celebrate?

Did you go through the motions of making a turkey at Thanksgiving because that's what you're "supposed" to do? Or did you celebrate? Did you delegate the turkey to your sister who loves roasting so you could bake your favorite pies, because you prefer baking? Did you intentionally take time with the people you were gathered with to express what you're thankful for, to ask and listen to what they're thankful for, and to praise God for all those things? Did you laugh and make merry? Or did you check cleaning, grocery shopping, and food prep off your list, then quickly clear the dishes and start washing them as soon as the last forkful of cranberries was set down?

When was the last time you celebrated something that wasn't on the calendar? It's important to make merry on special days like birthdays and holidays, but it's also awesome to pause on a weeknight to celebrate your win at work, the success of the event you planned, the start of something new, your team's victory, or National Doughnut Day. Both annual celebrations and in-the-moment celebrations are important ways to notice how good our God is.

Celebrations are important ways to notice how good our God is.

Because if we don't pause and celebrate, don't actually allow ourselves to slow down and enjoy the celebrations, then we're just on that treadmill trying to get to the next thing and the next. We're not fully noticing what God is doing for us, not fully receiving the gifts He's giving us. When we slow down enough to celebrate, we remember how good God is and what He provides, and we allow ourselves to more fully experience His goodness. We let the good thing—the step forward, the award, the fresh start—truly sink in.

Theologian Richard Foster says, "Celebration is central to all the Spiritual Disciplines. Without a joyful spirit of festivity the Disciplines become dull, death-breathing tools in the hands of modern Pharisees. Every Discipline should be characterized by carefree gaiety and a sense of thanksgiving."[1]

Well, that sounds fun. All these practices we're talking about adding to our lives (Sabbath, silence, fasting, prayer) should be carefree and filled with gratitude? Let's do it!

Philosopher and professor Dallas Willard said in regard to the feasts God instituted for the ancient Israelites, "Those feasts and celebrations are about training for joy."[2] God designed celebrations so we could get better at joy? God wants us to improve our capacity for having fun and enjoying life? I keep telling you: He's a really good God.

Who or what can you celebrate today? A family member's anniversary of being sober? The first snowfall? The last day of school? A new kitten?

If you're a booklover, you could host a book release party when your favorite author's latest title comes out, invite all your bookish friends, and make snacks that revolve around the book's theme. Maybe that's just a me thing. If you're a sports fan or a music lover, you could throw a Super Bowl or Grammy Awards party. Everyone could dress in the gear of their favorite team or as their favorite musician, celebrating these things that bring you joy. You could organize a fall fest and invite neighbors for a bonfire, celebrating pumpkins and leaves and sweater weather. Or have a game night or cookie baking night with family. You could celebrate the end of the semester or the end of tax season or the end of soccer season by going out for fajitas. You could have a celebration simply for the sake of celebrating—because God is always up to something good!

Being physically apart from your people doesn't have to get in the way of celebrating with them. My daughter who lives in Nashville had cookies delivered to our doorstep on my birthday, because she couldn't be with me. For a season our family had weekly "Games with Grandma." We'd Zoom my mom, who lives two and a half hours away, and play a game with her like Scattergories or Charades. We could see her and talk to her and giggle at our crazy antics. We celebrated family and our love for each other even though we couldn't be together. Neither of these things were fancy or hard to plan, but they were wonderful ways to celebrate even when we couldn't do it in person.

Celebrations don't have to be expensive or elaborate. Sure, they can be a ritzy dinner out with a champagne toast—or they can be the clanging of a cymbal with a borrowed drumstick. Celebration is simply recognizing something good God's done and delighting in it with others.

In 2 Samuel 6:5, King David sets a great example for us: "David and all Israel were celebrating with all their might before the Lord, with castanets, harps, lyres, timbrels, sistrums and cymbals." He was celebrating with all his might—full force, all out. You noticed there were cymbals, right? We can do this too. Get creative. Go for it. Jesus wants joy for us. He's literally encouraging us to take a break and enjoy this life with the people who matter most to us.

Don't just say, "Hey, we finished the Turkey Trot. That was fun. Glad we finished." Instead, eat the free red velvet cupcakes with cream cheese frosting from the local bakery at the finish line, and clang the cymbals along the route!

Slow Down

> David and all Israel were celebrating with all their might before the Lord, with castanets, harps, lyres, timbrels, sistrums and cymbals. (2 Samuel 6:5)

Who or what can you celebrate this week?

Write out how you plan to celebrate. Will there be snacks? Decorations? Who will be there? Where will you be?

Find a way to weave thanking God into your celebration. That could be a prayer or having everyone thank God out loud for this occasion or that person.

CHAPTER 23

Ducking into a Cathedral

Slowing Down on the Go

"It looks like maybe three more blocks this way?" My son looked up from the map of Washington, DC, we'd gotten at our hotel desk and squinted in the bright July sun.

Our destination for the day, the National Museum of American History, was located along the Mall. Not a mall where you shop, but the National Mall bookended by the United States Capitol and the Lincoln Memorial. We were headed in the right direction, but barricades, orange cones, and four construction workers in bright yellow helmets made it impossible for us to continue along our path.

"Okay, let's cross here and walk parallel that way." I pointed to where we could reroute toward our destination.

Maguire and I scurried away from the construction and across the street, where we found ourselves in front of a beautiful old church. Its doors were open, so we ducked inside.

The streets of the city had been abuzz with tourists and taxis, but inside it was as if someone had pushed the mute button and all sounds had been hushed. The building smelled like wood polish and slate, like decades of worship had taken place within these walls. Sunlight filtered in daintily through the stained glass windows, projecting a misty, muted glow across the rows of dark wooden pews and gray stone floors. Scaffolding that looked like it was made of brass zigzagged across the vaulted ceiling, and proud silver pipes stood upright in rows, ready to belt out the chords of the organ should someone strike its keys. The white altar was intricately carved, and the centerpiece—an arched stained glass masterpiece—adorned the wall behind the altar.

The building was filled with the type of slow, empty quiet that draws you to sit for a moment and pray. We slid into a pew, hard and solid, and closed our eyes. I inhaled the peace. The stillness. And I prayed.

I thanked God for this trip, this time with my boy, sunshine, the time and resources to make it all possible. I thanked God for each member of our family and prayed for them individually—for the needs I knew they had and the ones I might not ever know about. I poured out some things to Jesus that had been skirting around the edges of my mind, that I hadn't had time to really think about, let alone discuss with Him. And I sat in the quiet, just absorbing God's love and listening to Him.

Sit in the quiet and just absorb God's love.

When I finally opened my eyes, Maguire was sitting peacefully next to me, wide-eyed, taking in the beauty of the building, the architecture, the history. I could tell he'd also found a moment with Jesus. Even though we were out of our normal routines and spaces, even though we were sharing a small hotel room in the city, we'd found silence, solitude, and a place to pray. Together.

Stopping in churches while traveling is something our family began doing over a dozen years ago while in Lyon, France. My husband worked at a university there one spring, and the kids and I were blessed to join him. As we explored Lyon, we stumbled upon gorgeous church after stunning cathedral, most of which had been built with levers and pulleys and strong hands long before construction vehicles existed or the United States was formed. We found something meaningful in these houses of worship in a foreign land. Their grandness and history nudged us to exhale whatever was on our minds and stand in awe. The unhurriedness of embracing the beauty and peace in those cathedrals, of talking with God as long as we liked, was priceless.

Discovering a way to find a moment of silence and stillness to process our thoughts with Jesus while the six of us felt like we were living on top of each other in France was a gift. And really important. It was exactly what we needed to reset even when we were totally out of our element. So we've continued the tradition.

Sure, we can pray anywhere, anytime. That's a really cool thing about God. Jesus doesn't make it hard to get in touch with Him. We can talk to God in our cars, on the subway, at the grocery, or while scrubbing sinks. Anytime we talk to God, it is good. Finding a little peace and quiet to chat with the Lord is really helpful for spiritual and mental health.

At home this is easier for me. I have reading my Bible and prayer time scheduled into my day. I often go on a run by myself or step into my closet away from everyone to find some silence and solitude. But while traveling? Things look different. I'm usually less in control of my schedule, whether that's because I'm navigating our entire family's preferences and needs on a vacation, or I'm working around meetings and events on a business trip, or maybe I'm trying to roll with my mom's routine when I visit her. When I'm not at home, it's often more difficult to find somewhere to be alone.

You?

How do we lean into the spiritual practices we've been talking about in this book to live a more abundant life when we're in a different environment? When we're out of step from our normal routine?

We get creative.

For me, that's seeking out churches. In an old downtown church, I'm able to access silence, solitude, and prayer—three of the things we're trying to make room for in our lives. There are tons of churches with open doors in most major cities. When I walk into a church, sit in a pew, and close my eyes, it's purposeful. I've declared to myself, "While I'm in this place, I'm going to seek Jesus."

It is refreshing. Renewing. Restorative.

It pushes pause on the world and all the buzzers in it, and tells them, "Not now. Because right now, I'm unavailable. Right now, I'm going to be still. I'm going to be quiet. I'm going to talk to Jesus. And this intentional time with Jesus is a priority for me."

"Jesus often withdrew to lonely places and prayed." (Luke 5:16)

Jesus was also a big fan of finding some quiet on the go. "But Jesus often withdrew to lonely places and prayed" (Luke 5:16).

The Greek word used for "lonely places" is *erémos*. It's translated as "solitary," "lonely," "desolate," or "uninhabited." Pretty self-explanatory. Despite what was going on around Him, Jesus intentionally pulled away from the fray to be with God.

Easy for Jesus, you might be saying. He didn't spend two hours every day driving kids to and from school. He wasn't running His own business. He wasn't working two jobs to make ends meet. He wasn't caring for His aging parent on top of His other responsibilities. It's not that easy to sneak off by yourself.

Maybe not. But let's just say that saving the world kept Jesus in fairly high demand. He empathizes with your situation. For context, let's peek at the previous verse: "Yet the news about him spread all the more, so that crowds of people came to hear him and to be healed of their sicknesses" (v. 15).

Word had gotten out about how awesome and powerful Jesus was. He went viral. Everyone was coming to see Him. Crowds wanted healing. And in all this frenzy, Jesus withdrew to pray. Wait, was Jesus ignoring the people? Turning a cold shoulder? Nope. He cared so much about people. In Luke 4, the chapter before this one, Jesus literally spent a full evening healing a giant crowd: "At sunset, the people brought to Jesus all who had various kinds of sickness, and laying his hands on each one, he healed them" (v. 40). On that day, everyone who was sick, *all* of them, were brought to Him. And Jesus healed each and every person. Which must have been a long, exhausting evening.

But on the day in Luke 5, presumably soon after, there was another crowd. Another throng of people who wanted to be healed. And even though Jesus was full of compassion, even though our Savior is a healer, even though He loved to heal people, Jesus also knew that in order to have the words to speak to the crowd, in order to have the energy to heal the sick and wounded, He needed quiet, alone time with God. Jesus knew this time of withdrawing

215

would rest, center, empower, and refresh Him to do the work God called Him to next.

In the verse immediately following Jesus going off to be alone, He is once again speaking to a large crowd and healing people (v.17).

It was a rhythm with Jesus.

Do the work God called Him to do.

Get alone with God.

Do more of God's work.

Withdraw to a quiet place.

Heal more people. Teach the good news.

Sneak off somewhere desolate.

Such a beautiful cadence.

The more we step into Christ's unforced rhythms of grace, the more they become our *rhythms.*

We can become more like Jesus. When we feel the benefits of things like silence, solitude, and prayer in our daily lives, we begin to crave them all the time. We appreciate the peace and hope and joy they bring us. We start to search for and discover more opportunities to integrate these practices into our lives. No matter what's going on. No matter where we are. The more we step into Christ's unforced rhythms of grace, the more they become *our* rhythms.

It gets trickier when things feel out of whack—when our kids have the flu and we spend all day (and most of the night) tending to them. When a friend gets a flat tire and we unexpectedly take a chunk of our afternoon to come to their rescue. When we move or work somewhere new and everything feels different. When we're sharing a cubicle or room. But it's never impossible to seek time with Jesus.

Which is why our family crosses the thresholds of churches in towns we don't live in. On family trips, we're together for days on end, sharing rooms and meals and adventures. Which is awesome. But also. During that time in Lyon, the six of us (well, seven for the week my mom joined us) lived in a tiny two-bedroom apartment. My husband and I slept on a sofa bed in the main room each night. The kids were small, needing lots of supervision, and we were basically always together. Even in a cathedral, we weren't by ourselves. But we had an understanding that we'd all do our own quiet thing there. And it worked. It refreshed and reset us.

So we've kept it up. On one of Brett's business trips to San Francisco. On an educational service trip to Guatemala. While walking through downtown Cincinnati. One Smith might gaze at a scene of Jesus holding a lamb, depicted in jewel-toned puzzle pieces of glass, grateful that our Good Shepherd holds and cares for us. Another Smith might bow her head in a pew, praying silently or whispering prayers. One of us might stare at a cross or hum a worship song, thanking Jesus for His sacrifice. Still another Smith might light a candle and pray for a specific person or thing that's been on his heart, watching the wispy smoke ascend upward, like our prayers.

It's a lovely opportunity to be quiet before God. Keep our eyes open to His love and grace. Pray for those things we keep telling people "I'll be praying for you." Unload or unwind some things that have us twisted in knots. Spend time talking with Jesus about the things we've only mentioned to Him in snippets.

And sometimes it's less spiritual than that. Maybe it's just a moment to take in some beauty. A pause for our busy brains. A much-needed quiet after constant conversation. An opportunity for our souls to catch up to our bodies, which are so often in motion.

Churches are a great way to find these moments of stillness and solitude. But there are other places where we can interject stillness in our days. There are chapels in hospitals and airports, quiet corners in libraries, bookstores, and coffee shops. Lobbies of office buildings and hotels often provide clusters of comfy chairs where you can withdraw from work or travel and sit still, staring out the window and chatting with God. The laundry room in the basement of an apartment building, hotel, or dorm is often peaceful too. Even that drive time while picking up your friend with the flat can be the perfect opportunity to seek the Lord in silence.

You'll have to find your own spaces. Find what works for you. Where you can be by yourself to find stillness with Jesus. You'll have to be intentional. But the discovery is part of the fun.

Maguire and I sat a bit more, until we both felt ready to leave. Had it been ten minutes? Forty? It didn't matter. Because it was exactly what our souls needed. We emerged into the bright sunlight of DC, refreshed, reset, and ready to find the museum and whatever else God had in store.

Slow Down

> But Jesus often withdrew to lonely places and prayed.
> (Luke 5:16)

How do you normally spend time with Jesus when you're at home and in your regular routine?

Do you have a strategy or system in place to intentionally seek God when you're out of your normal place and space?

Do you have any upcoming situations —a trip, a house full of visitors, a demanding season at work—where it will be harder for you to seek silence and solitude?

Take a minute to brainstorm some ways you'll be able to find time alone with God during that situation. Put a note in your calendar on those days, reminding yourself of some of the ideas.

CHAPTER 24

Running around Central Park

Go Your Own Pace

My husband had a business trip to New York and flights were dirt cheap, so our youngest son, Maguire, and I tagged along. We're all runners, and if you're in New York City, Central Park is *the* place to run. We took the uptown train to the southwest corner of the park and tried to figure out how we were going to route our runs.

Maguire runs cross-country for his high school team and is speedy. Brett is faster than me by over a minute per mile. And me? Well, I run slower than both of them but at a pace and distance I'm proud of for a gal in her mid-fifties. Also, the park is huge with a myriad of paths. None of us are New Yorkers, and we didn't want to lose each other.

There is a large loop that goes around the park where loads of folks were cruising. I have zero sense of direction, and although I prefer a meandering trail, I suggested we run the loop. "Why don't we all go at our own pace? None of us can get lost. And we'll all meet back here when we're finished."

"I'll run with you," my husband said, always looking out for the safety of our family. "Maguire, you can go ahead. Mom and I will meet you back here."

"Go on." I nudged Brett. "I'll be fine. It's a circle." I grinned. "Even I can navigate that."

Brett surveyed the situation. "There are a lot of people. It feels pretty safe. Are you sure? Do you feel safe?"

"Totally safe. You'll get frustrated if you have to go my pace." I laughed. "And I can't keep up with yours."

"Okay. You sure?"

"Positive."

And so, the three of us each took off at our own pace.

Soon I found my cadence, and as I ran, it struck me that everyone at the park had a pace they were supposed to be moving at—not anyone else's but theirs. The large group of women that sped right past me from the get-go. The older gentleman pushing his disabled friend around the park in his wheelchair. The girl in the hot-pink skirt and matching lipstick and black-and-white polka-dot top. The fit guy in his fifties with the prosthetic leg. The dude speaking in French on his phone. The two gals chattering in Spanish as they walked. The men riding their bikes and conversing in Italian. All the people speaking languages I couldn't identify. Maguire. Brett. Me. We were all moving at our own pace. Because that's how we thrive.

Not only in Central Park. But in our lives.

God has plans and a purpose for all of us (Jeremiah 29:11). He wants goodness for you and me. But her pace and his pace are not necessarily my best pace or yours. Or they might be our pace for another time but not for this season now. Just because they have their degree, are married, started their own business, had a baby, and you haven't or don't doesn't mean you're behind. Not if you're walking at the pace God leads you.

As long as you're tracking with God and His plans for you, you are right on time.

As long as you're tracking with God and His plans for you, you are right on time.

We see God inviting people into the pace He has for them throughout Scripture. He promised two different women—Sarah and Mary—that they would have very important sons. Sarah had to wait and wait and wait. She and Abraham waited twenty-five years from the time God first promised them kids to when their son, Isaac, was born. Sarah was ninety! We're told how frustrated she was by this slow pace as she tried to take things into her own hands (Genesis 16:1–2) and even laughed at God (18:12) during the waiting. The Bible doesn't tell us why Sarah and Abraham had to wait. Was it to grow their trust, strengthen their faith, or coordinate other happenings with other people that would later affect Isaac? I don't know. But I do know that God's timing was perfect. He always knew it would take that long. And there was purpose in His pace.

Compare that to Mary's story. God sent the angel Gabriel to tell Mary she was going to have a baby—and shazam! She was pregnant (Luke 1:30–32). She was an unwed teenage girl and barely had time to blink or shop for maternity clothes. She might have preferred a moment to process everything at a slower pace.

Sarah waited. Mary didn't have time to catch her breath. And God's timing was perfect for both of them. He fulfilled His promises, as He always does. Both women had the sons God promised them when the time was right. For them.

God also had different speeds in store for Saul and David. God instructed the prophet Samuel to anoint both of these men as kings of Israel, but look at how each king's story played out.

When Samuel anointed Saul, he gave Saul instructions, then gathered the people and said, "'Do you see the man the LORD has chosen? There is no one like him among all the people.' Then the people shouted, 'Long live the king!'" (1 Samuel 10:24). And just like that, Saul was king. Was Saul ready? Did he wish he could prepare some more? There had never been a king in Israel before. What exactly was he supposed to do?

And David? Well . . . it started out similarly for him. "So Samuel took the horn of oil and anointed him in the presence of his brothers, and from that day on the Spirit of the LORD came powerfully upon David" (16:13). But from the time Samuel anointed David to when he took the throne? It was probably about fifteen years. Fifteen years of waiting while King Saul was still reigning but David knew he was going to be king. Fifteen years of fleeing King Saul, who was extremely jealous and dangerous and was trying to kill David. David might have wanted to speed things up, but God knew all along David was going to have to wait.

We don't always understand God's timing. We might never understand why that position or life stage came so quickly for one of our friends or peers but took *forever* for us. Maybe God needed to grow us. Maybe He needed to teach us some things. Maybe He wanted to make sure we didn't get out of breath. And we might not be sure why we got thrust into a certain responsibility or role without much preparation. Maybe God knew we were ready, or He needed something to happen, and that speedy pace got things in motion when they needed to be. Maybe God knew we'd actually enjoy running at a moderate pace or a faster one, and He orchestrated it that way simply for our long-term joy.

The more we live in God's unforced rhythms of grace, the more we take out the things that clutter our lives so we can be more in tune with Jesus, the better we'll be able to determine what pace He wants us to go in this season or for that project. Is this a season of rest or for meticulously learning a skill? If so, we can go s-l-o-w, no matter how fast everyone around us is going. Or is it go time? If so, let's charge ahead, refueled by the practices we've been intentionally packing in our bags.

The more we live in God's unforced rhythms of grace, the better we'll be able to determine what pace He wants us to go in this season.

Should you try to get pregnant now? Or wait? Should you create a profile on that dating app? Or savor your singleness? Should you apply for a new position? Are you ready yet? Should you brush up on your skills first? Take a few classes? Is it time to speak up? Or should you bite your tongue one more day?

I don't have the answers for you. But God does. He has a time and pace for everything and everyone.

> To everything there is a season,
> A time for every purpose under heaven:
>
> A time to be born,
> And a time to die;

A time to plant,
And a time to pluck what is planted;
A time to kill,
And a time to heal;
A time to break down,
And a time to build up;
A time to weep,
And a time to laugh;
A time to mourn,
And a time to dance;
A time to cast away stones,
And a time to gather stones;
A time to embrace,
And a time to refrain from embracing;
A time to gain,
And a time to lose;
A time to keep,
And a time to throw away;
A time to tear,
And a time to sew;
A time to keep silence,
And a time to speak;
A time to love,
And a time to hate;
A time of war,
And a time of peace.

(Ecclesiastes 3:1–8 NKJV)

If you're slowing down enough to listen to His voice, spending time in prayer, finding some pauses and quiet in your life, worshipping the God who made you, you'll be better able to sense what pace God is setting for you.

It's hard to remember sometimes. Especially when we see others speeding past. But just like I knew if I tried to keep pace with

Maguire or Brett, I'd run out of gas before I ever finished the loop in Central Park, the same holds true on our life journeys. Not to mention when we rush things, we'll miss some of the beauty God has for us along the way.

That day in Central Park, Maguire texted us when he hit the five-mile mark to check in. Soon after Brett also texted that he'd logged five miles so far. I was behind them, but I didn't care. As Brett's text was coming in, I spotted a gorgeous waterfall to my left. I slowed down to veer off the pavement and took a closer look. I snapped a picture, listened to the roar of the water, and breathed in a moment of peace. As I pivoted to get back on track, another woman saw me and slowed her gait to gaze at the falls.

"It's beautiful, isn't it?" I asked.

"It really is," she marveled.

My slowing down gave her permission to slow down. That wasn't my intent. But what a lovely side effect. We can do this for each other. Go at our own pace, the pace God has for each of us, and in doing so invite others to do the same.

As I was coming down the west side of the park toward where we'd all started, Brett and Maguire stood cheering for me. They were clapping and yelling, "Go, Mom!" And I felt so loved. So valued.

They never once judged me because I was slower than them. They were proud of me for running my race.

If this is how my husband and son love me, can you imagine how much more God loves us? Cheers for us when we go at the pace He intends for us?

If God tells me to slow down, I want to rest and recover and be renewed. I want to see and learn what He has for me, so when God calls me to kick into gear, I'll be refueled and ready and raring to go.

God has good plans for you! Big loops, record speeds,

strengthening for your trust muscles, slow runs, cardio workouts that will get your heart pumping, peaceful pauses, and stunning waterfalls. And when you go at His pace, you'll experience the fullness and richness He planned for you all along.

Run your race.

At your God-led pace.

I'm cheering for you.

And so is Jesus.

Slow Down

> To everything there is a season,
> A time for every purpose under heaven.
> (Ecclesiastes 3:1 NKJV)

What in your current season is taking longer than you hoped or going faster than you planned?

Ask Jesus to help you understand His pace for you. Thank Him for His perfect timing and purpose, and ask Him to help you go the speed He's planned for you.

Does anyone come to mind who has been waiting or who feels like their life is on fast-forward? Shoot them a message or give them a call to tell them you're cheering for them.

Conclusion
Why Was This So Urgent?

Why again is it so urgent to slow down? The first chapter seems like a while ago. Do you feel like you just got a list of things you need to add to your life? Say no to things, make sure you celebrate, take time to pray, read your Bible . . . Um, when? Are you not sure how to create these new rhythms as you struggle to swear off work one day a week and also somehow spend less time on social media?

That wasn't the point.

Early on we talked about how our lives are like bags, and we get to choose how we fill them. We can fill them with things that cave to the demands of the world, that make us spin like tops, leaving us dizzy. We can fill them with things that we're holding on to because we don't trust God, or because we want to elevate our status, or because we've always had them or done things that way. *Or* we can empty out all the things that no longer help or grow us. We still have the same bag with the same capacity to hold the same total amount of stuff. But now that there's some room in there, we can choose to refill our bags with love, joy, peace, patience, kindness, goodness, faithfulness, gentleness, and self-control—the fruit of the Spirit (Galatians 5:22–23).

We get all these things when we intentionally seek time with

Jesus. We become filled with the Holy Spirit and all the fruit that comes with Him. When we pause to get quiet with Jesus, read His living Word, seek His advice and guidance, this spiritual fruit grows and grows. Then on days when bad things happen, we still find ourselves able to find joy. In the midst of a stressful situation, we are flooded with an inexplicable peace that surpasses all understanding. We find ourselves less tempted by things we used to cave to and more interested in things that fill us with goodness. Getting rid of the things that hog our time and distract us from Jesus frees up space for us to notice and appreciate the goodness and love that follow us all of our days (Psalm 23:6).

I began my journey of slowing down in 2019. Our lives were hurried. Jam-packed. A slower way of life sounded dreamy but difficult to obtain. My first step was trying to implement Sabbath. I thought maybe I could slow down for part of one day a week. And then it evolved into so much more. I found that the more I intentionally slowed down, the more the noise of the world turned down. And I was able to hear God and His call on my life more clearly.

Oddly, I seemed to still be getting all the important things done. How could that be?

I think it was two things. First, eliminating some things that were wastes of my time allowed me more time for things that truly mattered to and delighted me. Second, my body, mind, and soul were more rested than they had been in a very long time, so they actually functioned better, more efficiently. When I wasn't exhausted or frazzled, I could write more clearly and be more focused. I could better remember details that needed tending to and things people shared with me. I was getting more done in less time. In the pauses, I was more present.

But my work isn't done. Part of what I've discovered is that I need to continue to assess how I use my time with each new season, opportunity, and responsibility. When recently asked to help lead a Bible study at my church, I needed to make room for it in my calendar by saying no to something else. When I decided to try spinning as a new form of exercise this year, I substituted spin class for one of the runs in my weekly routine. As I tried to implement a daily prayer time, I discovered that when I have a regular time I shoot for, I'm way more consistent than when I just try to pray "sometime" during the day. When I downloaded an app to improve my Italian, the notifications distracted me. I got caught up in the points I could earn on the app instead of focusing on learning Italian. I had to make myself delete that app and come up with a new plan. Now I listen to an Italian podcast when I have extra time, but it doesn't keep score, distract me with notifications, or keep me on my phone.

I haven't perfected all this. I'm still learning for sure. But I'm making progress.

This slower life is a more abundant life.

And honestly, this slower life is a more abundant life. I believe it's a gift God is giving me and wants to give you. When we follow Him, when we try to live more like Jesus, it's ours for the taking. Jesus said, "I have come that they may have life, and have it to the full" (John 10:10).

This full life is waiting for you. It's not out of reach. All you have to do is slow down to make time for Jesus.

Incorporating these practices into our daily lives, slowing down and remembering who God is, what He does, and who He says we are—these things change our entire point of view. For the better. And I pray this change in us will be visible. That the world sees the difference between us and our frantic culture. I pray we'll be obviously more rested, less frazzled, more at peace, and more content with what we have. We won't need to strive or acquire to prove ourselves. Because we'll remember that we have the applause of heaven. That Jesus loves us right now, not because of our accomplishments but simply because He does.

When we follow Him more closely, live in line with how He lived, and spend less time immersed in jam-packed homes, feeds, and schedules, our lights can shine brighter.

Jesus told His disciples in Matthew 5:14–16, "You are the light of the world. A town built on a hill cannot be hidden. Neither do people light a lamp and put it under a bowl. Instead they put it on its stand, and it gives light to everyone in the house. In the same way, let your light shine before others, that they may see your good deeds and glorify your Father in heaven." Jesus calls us to let our lights shine. When we follow Him more closely, live in line with how He lived, and spend less time immersed in jam-packed homes, feeds, and schedules, our lights can shine brighter. Not because of something we're doing, but because Jesus's light naturally emanates from us when we clear that clutter out of the way.

I want to be a person who has time to hold the door open for the person behind me because I'm not in a rush. I want to be the mama who listens to my kids, not looking down at my phone but directly in their eyes. I want to be the girl who enjoys the food and experiences in front of me, not the one who shoves it all down, barely tasting or noticing it. I want to feel rested and refreshed so I can do the work God calls me to do well. I want to feel like I have love to give because I'm coming from a place of fullness, not depletion.

Me? I'm going to try my best to let this little light shine.

Jesus invites us to follow Him into His rhythms of work and play, going and stopping, celebrating with others and quietly going off by ourselves to seek Him.

Slow down and exhale. Get rid of the junk. Free up your calendar and brain for more time—time with the One who loves you and longs to save you.

Then, rested, refueled, and reset, go shine. Go shine to the world.

Acknowledgments

Jesus, I never want to be too busy for you. It is your amazing grace that saved me and your love that sustains me. Thank you. I pray I always slow down to be with you, because when I do, everything is brighter and more beautiful.

Brett, thank you for embarking on a journey of discovering God's unforced rhythms of grace with me. I love slowing down with you to go on walks, chat by the fire, talk over coffee, travel, laugh—all of it. I'd stop the world to melt with you.

To my four kids—slowing down with you makes me a better person, makes me more myself, shows me beautiful reflections of God in each of you.

Maddie, I love slowing down with you to explore bookstores and coffee shops, go for strolls on the beach, bake cookies, try new restaurants, giggle about hedgehogs, or simply chat about our days.

Max, I love slowing down to talk to you about Jesus and how He is alive and active in our lives and in the world, and about how His ways are always better.

Mallory, I love slowing down with you to have picnics on the family room floor, dip strawberries in chocolate, go on road trips, and share silly stories.

Maguire, I love slowing down with you to go on adventures, discuss social justice, go to the zoo, or watch Marvel movies.

Mom, I love slowing down with you to hear about your life, play cards, and spend precious moments with you.

Thank you to my incredible team at Our Daily Bread Publishing. Your hearts for Jesus, your willingness to build the kingdom, and your kindness are such a blessing. Thank you for making time for me and for this important message of how urgent it is for us to slow down. Specifically, Joel Armstrong, you are a rock star editor. This book is a million times better because of your insights and suggestions. Thank you! J.R. Hudberg, your biblical knowledge was integral in making sure these pages honor God's living Word. Dawn Anderson, your continuous support and partnership mean the world to me (this is our fourth book together!). Sarah De Mey, thank you for coordinating all the pieces. Melissa Wade, I cannot thank you enough for all the endless tasks you do and creative ideas you have and execute that help get these words out into the world. Kat Needham, thank you for getting the message of *The Urgency of Slowing Down* into so many people's hands. Patti Brinks, I am in love with this cover! Thank you for making everyone's first impression of this book a gorgeous one. Linnae Conkel, thank you for your attention to detail. Cathy Sall, your behind-the-scenes work does not go unnoticed. Chriscynethia Floyd, you make it all possible. I'm grateful for all of you.

Bob Hostetler, thank you for your guidance and support, for listening to me gush about the books God has placed on my heart to write and then helping me find homes for those books to become realities.

Amy, you have talked me through and encouraged me along every single book I've written, including this one. But even more valuable than your advice and cheerleading is your true, loyal, priceless friendship.

Shena, meeting you in Bible study is one of my greatest joys.

You are so dear to me. Thank you for helping me process all the ways Jesus is on the move.

Tammy, your sweet, genuine, beautiful heart, soul, and self is a precious gift.

Playlist

. . . speaking to one another with psalms, hymns, and songs from
the Spirit. Sing and make music from your heart to the Lord.

Ephesians 5:19

Music can reduce stress, strengthen the immune system, and
improve mood. We're also instructed throughout the Bible
to sing unto the Lord. Which makes me very happy, because I
am a music lover. Music is always a part of my process. And so,
I've put together a playlist of the songs that resonated with my
heart and soul as I wrote *The Urgency of Slowing Down*.

You can find these songs and others on Spotify on the "Urgency of Slowing Down" playlist by laurasmithauthor, or I've
listed many songs below so you can access them however you
listen to music.

"Wait on You" by Elevation Worship and Maverick City Music
"The 59th Street Bridge Song (Feelin' Groovy)" by Simon &
    Garfunkel
"Endless Alleluia" by Cory Asbury
"Give Me Jesus" by UpperRoom
"Give Me Jesus" by Shane & Shane
"Word of God Speak" by MercyMe

"Full Attention" by Jeremy Riddle

"Raise a Hallelujah" by Bethel Music, Jonathan David Helser, and Melissa Helser

"This Is the Kingdom" by Elevation Worship featuring Pat Barrett

"This Love" by Housefires

"Abandoned" by Benjamin William Hastings and Brandon Lake

"As You Find Me" by Hillsong United

"Rest on Us" by Maverick City Music and UpperRoom

"Nothing Else" by Cody Carnes

"Lean Back" by Maverick City Music and Chandler Moore

"Take Courage" by Kristene DiMarco and Bethel Music

"Dear God" by Cory Asbury

"Crashing In" by Cory Asbury

"Voice of Truth" by Casting Crowns

"Came to My Rescue" by Hillsong United

"This Little Light of Mine" by Rend Collective

"The Heart of Worship" by Matt Redman

"Build My Life" by Housefires

"Everything" by Lifehouse

"Thank You Song" by UpperRoom

"The Lord's Prayer (It's Yours)" by Matt Maher

"Turn! Turn! Turn! (To Everything There Is a Season)" by The Byrds

"Honestly, We Just Need Jesus" by Terrian

"That's the Thing about Praise" by Benjamin William Hastings and Blessing Offor

"Kinda Wild" by Judah and Ellie Holcomb

"Rest" by TobyMac, Terrian, and Gabe Real

"You Saved Me + Spontaneous" by FM Worship and Maxwell Smith

Notes

Chapter 6: The Art of Saying No

1. Natalie Harris-Spencer, "21 Debut Author Statistics: The Real Odds of Getting Published," Aspiring Author, last modified March 6, 2023, https://aspiringauthor.com /publishers/statistics-odds-of-getting-published/.

Chapter 7: How Much Is Enough?

1. "Take Back Your Garage: American Garages Store More Clutter than Cars, According to Craftsman Survey," PR Newswire, November 1, 2022, https://www.prnewswire .com/news-releases/take-back-your-garage-american -garages-store-more-clutter-than-cars-according-to -craftsman-survey-301664129.html.

Chapter 8: What Sloths Can Teach Us

1. Sharyn Alfonsi, "Sloths, the World's Slowest Mammal, Turn Survival of the Fittest Upside Down," *60 Minutes*, CBS News, last modified December 24, 2023, https:// www.cbsnews.com/news/sloths-survival-worlds-slowest -mammal-60-minutes-transcript/.
2. "9 Ways to Slow Down and Enjoy Life More," Ramsey Solutions, January 3, 2024, https://www.ramseysolutions .com/personal-growth/the-beauty-of-slowing-down.

Chapter 9: Off the Grid

1. Paul Lewis, "'Our Minds Can Be Hijacked': The Tech Insiders Who Fear a Smartphone Dystopia," *Guardian*, October 6, 2017, https://www.theguardian.com /technology/2017/oct/05/smartphone-addiction-silicon -valley-dystopia.
2. *The Social Dilemma*, directed by Jeff Orlowski (Boulder, CO: Exposure Labs, 2020).
3. *The Social Dilemma*.

Part 2: Refuel

1. David Shimer, "Yale's Most Popular Class Ever: Happiness," *New York Times*, January 26, 2018, https://www .nytimes.com/2018/01/26/nyregion/at-yale-class-on -happiness-draws-huge-crowd-laurie-santos.html.
2. Resources from Dr. Laurie Santos: "The Science of Well-Being," Coursera, accessed March 4, 2024, https://www .coursera.org/learn/the-science-of-well-being; "The Science of Well-Being," DrLaurieSantos.com, accessed March 4, 2024, https://www.drlauriesantos.com/science-well-being.

Chapter 11: Quiet Time

1. Sarah Garone, "8 Physical and Mental Health Benefits of Silence, Plus How to Get More of It," Healthline, last modified September 24, 2021, https://www.healthline .com/health/mind-body/physical-and-mental-health -benefits-of-silence.

Chapter 14: Friday Mornings

1. Jill Suttie, "How Music Bonds Us Together," *Greater Good Magazine*, June 28, 2016, https://greatergood.berkeley

.edu/article/item/how_music_bonds_us_together. See also Rebecca Joy Stanborough, "10 Ways That Singing Benefits Your Health," Healthline, November 10, 2020, https:// www.healthline.com/health/benefits-of-singing.

2. Tim Keller, "The Song of Creation," Gospel in Life, October 15, 2000, https://gospelinlife.com/sermon /the-song-of-creation/.

Chapter 16: How Long Should You Look at a Sunset?

1. Elizabeth Hutton Turner, *Georgia O'Keeffe: The Poetry of Things* (New Haven, CT: Yale University Press, 1999), 47.

Chapter 17: Shake Mistakes

1. Thomas A. Tarrants, "The Place of Fasting in the Christian Life," C. S. Lewis Institute, June 6, 2018, https:// www.cslewisinstitute.org/resources/the-place-of-fasting -in-the-christian-life/.

2. Tarrants, "The Place of Fasting in the Christian Life."

3. Jonathan Outlaw, "Survey Finds Disordered Eating Behaviors among Three out of Four American Women," The University of North Carolina at Chapel Hill, April 22, 2008, https://uncnewsarchive.unc.edu/2008/04/22 /survey-finds-disordered-eating-behaviors-among-three -out-of-four-american-women-2/.

Chapter 18: It's Just Practice

1. Tim Keller, "How We Live as Believers," Gospel in Life, September 27, 2019, https://podcast.gospelinlife.com/e /how-we-live-as-believers/.

Chapter 19: Charcuterie To Go

1. Anne Lamott, *Small Victories: Spotting Improbable Moments of Grace* (New York: Riverhead Books, 2014), 100.
2. A. Elizabeth Sloan, "What, When, and Where America Eats," Institute of Food Technologists, January 1, 2020, https://www.ift.org/news-and-publications/food-technology-magazine/issues/2020/january/features/what-when-and-where-america-eats.

Chapter 20: Magic Spot

1. "3 Ways Getting Outside into Nature Helps Improve Your Health," UC Davis Health, May 3, 2023, https://health.ucdavis.edu/blog/cultivating-health/3-ways-getting-outside-into-nature-helps-improve-your-health/2023/05.

Chapter 22: Cymbals and Drumsticks

1. Richard J. Foster, *Celebration of Discipline: The Path to Spiritual Growth* (New York: HarperCollins, 1998), 191.
2. Dallas Willard, *Living in Christ's Presence: Final Words on Heaven and the Kingdom of God* (Downers Grove, IL: InterVarsity Press, 2013), 146.

Also available from Laura L. Smith

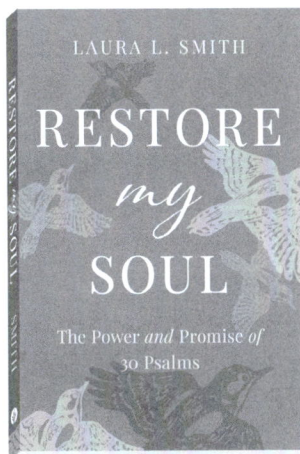

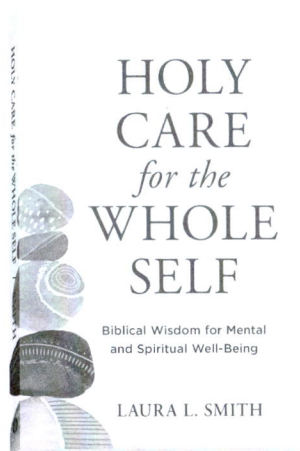

LAURA L. SMITH

RESTORE
my
SOUL

The Power *and* Promise *of*
30 Psalms

HOLY
CARE
for the
WHOLE
SELF

Biblical Wisdom for Mental
and Spiritual Well-Being

LAURA L. SMITH

Spread the Word
by Doing One Thing.

- Give a copy of this book as a gift.
- Share the QR code link via your social media.
- Write a review of this book on your blog, favorite bookseller's website, or at ODB.org/store.
- Recommend this book to your church, small group, or book club.

Our Daily Bread.

Connect with us. f ⓘ

Our Daily Bread Publishing
PO Box 3566, Grand Rapids, MI 49501, USA
Email: books@odb.org

Love God. Love Others.

with 🖤 Our Daily Bread®

Your gift changes lives.

Connect with us. 🅕 🅞

Our Daily Bread Publishing
PO Box 3566, Grand Rapids, MI 49501, USA
Email: books@odb.org